Rogue Capitalist: The exclusive guide to navigating the New Normal & The Great Reset

Johann Loke

Copyright © 2022 Johann Loke

All Rights Reserved

ISBN: 978-981-18-6404-9

DEDICATION

To my family, my loved ones, and those who have been with me
since day one. You know who you are.

CONTENTS

CHAPTER 1: THE ROGUE'S PATH

The first sentence of a book is often the toughest. I had to rewrite this chapter twice; the same amount of times the title changed. The original plan was to go with the "Accidental Entrepreneur." However, upon finishing the final chapter of this book, I made the last change to the title. The title "Rogue Capitalist" was a decision made upon a belief system known as capitalism that ran through my veins - something close to what my ancestors had embraced in pursuit of a better life for their families. The "Rogue" part came from the path taken as a youth, thrown into the depths of intense competition from seven years old. While other children enjoyed their time running around in playgrounds, having cheeky pecks on their cheeks, and eating hotdogs, mine was spent in solitary silence practicing the Chinese flute (dizi). Shouldering the wishes and dreams of my primary school seniors to bag the gold medal for my primary school's Chinese Orchestra, it became my goal to accomplish it for them.

These seniors eventually went on to secondary school. Me being nine at the time and halfway through my primary school tenure, I was left all alone - the dream of a gold medal solely entrusted to me. I couldn't remember smiling that much growing up; as a young boy entrusted with an impossible task. Lucky for me, I was blessed to have had a supportive family and to live in a neighborhood filled with esteemed individuals. They never once told me to give up and would allow me to perform with my dizi in front of them. The gold medal dream never came to fruition as I approached my final year in primary school. I was devastated by it and decided to give up on playing music. I realized early on that I could not achieve things alone; my peers in primary school still treated the Chinese Orchestra as an after-school fun activity of playing music with their classmates. It's the kind of thing to expect when dealing with children. My focus and determination didn't waver then. Somehow I knew that anything I wanted to accomplish was within my reach as long as I put my heart and soul into it.

They say that three things make a man.

The blood in his veins - the legacy of his bloodline.

The homeland of his.

The bonds he made in his lifetime.

To know what an individual is capable of may seem like an esoteric belief. Talents and traits don't magically appear instantly - it often takes years for them to manifest. Growing up, I would regularly probe my parents about my grandparent's history. They left this realm before I was born, leaving me curious about who they were and what they did. Being fascinated by history, especially ancient Egyptian history (from the card game I played professionally - Yu-Gi-Oh!), made me ask questions about what my grandparents did in the past. My parents were Chefs - getting acquainted and married through their profession. My father is Chef Simon Loke, a highly respected man in his profession based on my experiences watching other Chefs interact with him. Having accompanied my father on several business trips, I saw firsthand how skilled in the culinary arts he was. His demeanor was very focused, often relying on his prowess and actions to speak for him. My mother is Abby Pang, the title of Chef not being bestowed to her as she left the culinary scene immediately after my elder sister was born. She spent her best years raising her children and only went back after we entered high school. Upon returning to the culinary scene, she walked into the MBS office and charmed the executive team within minutes. The team immediately gave her a job as a key player on their culinary team. After several years in MBS (Marina Bay Sands), she left and moved to the newly christened Singapore Sports Hub. She is known as an outspoken and attractive lady, a precious commodity in F&B, usually dominated by male talents.

Knowing my parent's lineage as Chefs didn't propel me to become a Chef. The thing I derived from their expertise is their competency in their skillset, something the general public lacked. I only recently found out about my grandparents - from both sides. From my paternal side, my grandfather was an incredibly calculated risk-taker. Having left Singapore before it became independent to seek riches in Malaysia by building a water pipeline, his gamble paid off, and he struck gold. My auntie would tell me stories of my paternal grandfather being the first man in Singapore to own a Mercedes Benz and a Television in the 1900s. While on my maternal side, my grandfather personally undertook the mission to go to Singapore alone from Hainan Island to set up a food business in the Singapore Island Country Club, together with the Hainanese Kong Xi Clan. After building up his capital and becoming a respected man in this new society, he never once forgot his promise of helping out his family and friends. He then got them on the boat to bring them to Singapore, providing accommodation and jobs to forge a better life there. Knowing these feats of accomplishments from my grandparents and the history of my bloodline gave me a sense of confidence and pride - if my ancestors before had achieved success, why can't I have the same success as well? They say that success often leaves clues in the past; this couldn't be more clear than this. I didn't accept capitalism at face value growing up. I lacked an understanding of the systems that society has. It was apparent my knowledge was lacking in certain areas. However, I knew my bloodline had ancestors who would achieve big things in life. The blood running through their veins was now running through mine. Before getting married and settling down, my father spent most of his career abroad. Always the first man to jump out of his comfort zone, he spent many years working in China, and Antigua, a country in the Caribbean Islands. The thought of having a family and returning to Singapore was not something he considered. Singapore in the 1970s and 1980s was not the best country to develop one's prowess in the culinary arts. To hone his craft, leaving this country for better pastures was the best play he could have made back then. Singapore in the 1990s was when things started to pick up. Our pioneer generation and the founding fathers finally saw the fruits of their labor. International businesses and entrepreneurs from all over the world turned their attention to this tiny red dot. This country saw an influx of capital flowing in, and with the existing policies favoring businesses, Singapore became the destination for these foreigners. My father received an offer from Singapore Airlines to return to Singapore and join them. At first, he was apprehensive - there was nothing he could learn from working in Singapore's F&B scene. However, he realized that after many years of honing his skills, its finally time for him to showcase and put them to use. Accepting SIA (Singapore Airlines) offer, he returned to his homeland as a veteran.

Shortly after that, my father married my mother and having a family was the next thing he wanted - after all that years of sacrifice away from home to attain wealth and status. I was born into a family where I didn't have to struggle with not having food on the table or shelter over my head. Many Singaporeans and their typical "Asian parent" tendency would force their child to study hard and get a good job. None of that happened during my time growing up. It was a complete 180 from the type of growing-up pains other Singaporean children had. My parents decided to give us the best chance in the world and the best environment possible. They bought a property in a private estate to allow us to grow up surrounded by other like-minded professionals and entrepreneurs who made it in the 1990s. My father spent little time with my family due to work commitments, often traveling abroad for food presentations. Whereas my mother would shower us with love and affection, spending all of her time nurturing us with a smile (and the occasional anger).

The neighbors I played in the playgrounds with became lifelong friends. Even though we spent our years in the public school education system, none of us would feel connected to our peers in school. Maybe it's a different type of upbringing? Or perhaps the kind of mentality instilled in us from the beginning? While our classmates were studying hard to get good grades, most of us played catching and blind mice. Playing the PlayStation, Xbox and latest Nintendo handheld consoles was an activity we enjoyed. There was one incident where I brought a Nintendo DS (the newest console) to school, and I was the student in my class who had it at the time. I felt it was odd being the only one who owned one. That was when the seeds of knowing my circumstances were different started to sprout in me. Then again, fast forward two decades later, and every child owns the latest iPad and iPhone. Singapore escalated quickly, and the luxuries my friends had when we were young have become normalized.

Walking down the streets of Singapore will be clean and proper. Foreigners were taking up jobs to clean up the streets as we sleep - to maintain the image of a green and clean city. It was a sign of a prosperous nation.

The image of Singapore is a result of the efficiencies of the Singaporean government and its ruling party - the People's Action Party. Singapore has a good reputation, especially when compared to other parts of SEA (Southeast Asia). At the time, most countries in SEA could be called third-world countries. There was nothing close to what Singapore had achieved in a short time, resulting in the country developing a psyche of never wanting to fail. Kiasu was used to describe it. Kiasu's official meaning is "having a grasping or selfish attitude arising from a fear of missing out on something" - in other words, not liking to lose. My classmates in school often showed this attitude, never wanting to suffer defeat at the hands of another regarding their grades. With this mentality growing up, it was no surprise to see Singaporeans having some success in the corporate sector - this is the perfect psyche needed to harm and push people out of their ways to climb the ladder of the rat race. Having a "Kiasu" mentality meant that embracing the spirit of capitalism in this country was not adopted by many - how could one possibly exist in a team with others without being able to compromise? One friend of mine would tell me how this "Kiasu" mentality would eventually become a double-edged sword, as his parents would narrate to him during dinnertime. I didn't pay much attention to this kiasu thing my classmates had. My goal was to play card games and become champion one day. Even my parents did not dissuade me from doing that - that was how different my upbringing was.

Knowing that the people growing up with me was the ones I could trust and was always there when I needed them was similar to the environment of the Kampung Spirit that Singapore had before it turned into the city as people know it today. This stark contrast between the bonds I made growing up versus the classmates I had in the public school education system was very wide when it came to aspirations and goals we had. The students I met all had the same canned response regarding what they wanted to achieve in life - often ranging from the usual lawyer and doctor talk - they had no control over what they wanted to be. My classmates didn't recognize my passion for music. Neither did they care much about my dream to become a champion one day. They were distracted by a belief system forced upon them. We were truly living in different worlds.

I was often bored by the same topics my classmates talked about as I progressed through secondary and then high school. I realized that the type of things I wanted to achieve and my worldview couldn't align with most Singaporeans. During this time, I started to spend less time with my peers in the school system and chose a life of playing card games professionally. Time spent on the weekend turned to competing in tournaments and aiming to win a cash prize. The cash prize would allow me to treat myself to a nice meal at a restaurant. By the time I was sixteen years old and about to finish secondary school, I had already achieved a lifestyle of eating Italian and Japanese food on weekends. While my friends were all drowning in the never-ending cycle of the mini rat race of homework, tuition, and exams. Here I was playing card games and focusing on my goals in life. There was a problem I identified as a teenager - most Singaporeans are copies of one another without anything interesting about themselves - they were all controlled based on the whims of an unseen power behind the scenes. Enjoying their youth was not an option. My analysis at the time was far ahead of my age group and warranted a reputation for being too cynical.

Due to my father's profession and international reputation, I often traveled overseas with him on his business trips. Being exposed to the world at such a young age did wonders for me. It broadened my worldview and allowed me to make friends with children his colleagues had in other parts of the world. In some parts of the world, I saw the living conditions of the people there. It wasn't the best sight to see. Whereas in other countries, life appears decent but nowhere close to what Singapore has. There was a sense of pride in being a Singaporean that I wore on me when talking to my international friends. Even to this day, I still keep in contact with these friends due to the lifestyle of being globally connected was something relatable. After my trips, I would bring back the camera my father brought along with us and have the photos processed. The process involved sending the entire reel to a photography shop and printing it in high quality. I would take the time to put the pictures into an album and share them with my neighbors. We would take turns whenever we had trips abroad to share our experiences. Nothing enriched our souls more than knowing what life is like overseas.

Whenever I tried to share albums with my classmates in the public school system, they were not receptive or interested. Probably caring more about another person's exam grades was more important to them. Eventually, I got the memo that they weren't interested in the world or culture abroad. That lesson expedited the process of making me lose interest in talking to my classmates. That left me with my neighbors, the ones I formed a bond with growing up. These classmates of mine would become adults one day. I could only imagine how they would be as one. Was it a sign of bad things to come?

As the world around us moved quickly, my neighbors and I realized that the Singapore we knew today did not resemble the one we knew. We noticed radical changes to the nation's psyche as time passed. Our neighbors started moving out one by one. Foreigners bought up the property next to ours. It is the sort of change that makes one feel something is amiss. When the original Singaporeans living in my estate left, and as more international people came in, the history and culture dissipated immediately. Festivals and celebrations we organized didn't take place any more. The international crowd did not participate in them and didn't care about my estate's culture. The facilities we had started to spoil more often. The language we spoke was no longer the same. We were still too young as teenagers to understand - was this a byproduct of the globalization we have? We made a vow on that day - no matter what happened to Singapore, we would still have each other backs until the end. The vow made me treasure the bonds I made with the ones who stuck by me. We still remember the days and the phone numbers of our homes. We exist, shouldering the memories of Singapore's past before it transformed into the modern dystopia of today.

With this moral inclination instilled in us, I decided to write this book as the changes that rapidly changed Singapore has finally reached the tipping point. The western influence we have been importing through the mainstream media is finally showing its true colors. The masses I predicted as a child to be copies of each other have been given the program to be assimilated into the hive mind as we speak.

The joke my neighbors and I had growing up about our beloved homeland going to the dumpster has finally arrived. This book will be a story about the trends which happened in the past and the evolution of my country's free markets turning into a centrally planned agenda machine.

Chapter 2: The Longest Holiday

For the majority of the readers of this book, it might be the first time you have heard about me. To another group of minorities who first knew me before reading this book, there was an identity and profession that has molded me into the person I am today - one rarely discussed today.

There was a time when I used to play card games professionally. It all started during secondary school. From time to time, joining and competing in card games began as a hobby. There was one particular run as a professional during my first year of polytechnic culminating in me winning a championship, topping multiple tournaments, and even representing Singapore at an international tournament with the best players representing their countries in attendance. As much as I would like to talk more about card games in this book, this should be a sufficient enough background to my backstory. Everything came to a crashing halt the day I turned eighteen years old; my father sat me down before I even cut my birthday cake. It was a delicious-looking dark chocolate cake he made for me. My father looked me in the eyes; the aura surrounding him - with time and space having distorted seemed to have stopped at that moment.

It was something unknown to me. For many years my father always treated me as a child. I knew on that day when I turned 18; that he wasn't just looking at his son anymore - my father looked at me with a look - one that any man would show another adult male.

"Johann, you turn 18 today. It is time for you to take responsibility and start making your own money. I will not be giving you any more pocket money."

It took me a long time to process this information. I never knew how to make money outside of the allowance given. Even when I played card games, it still required stimulus from my father to keep it up. My life since birth was a by-product of my father's guiding hand, allowing me to enjoy the world's pleasures without labor. My professional card game career was no longer possible without money coming in - that being the first thing that crossed my mind. Heck, there's no way that my bubble tea addiction could be satisfied without it too. My mind went into overdrive to think of ways to fix this problem. During the last school holidays, I spent it working at the nearby supermarket as my parents always wanted me to have some experience outside of the school system. The experience taught me a lot about how a supermarket functions as a business and when was the best time to visit them to buy the freshest fruits. However, there wasn't much to learn from working in a supermarket. I had an itch that wanted more, a more fulfilling experience that could satisfy my curiosity. Then and there, I decided to try out working in the F&B industry. The very same industry my parents were involved in, where they paved their legacies and carved a name for themselves.

I remember being angry and confused about what my father did. A decade has passed since that day. Looking back, It remains one of the pivotal moments that helped me wake up from the illusion. The illusion that money is free. Someone needs to produce to attain currency units - in that case, legal tender notes - money.

The first order of business was to sell some of the trading cards that were in my collection. Surprisingly, the thing about playing physical card games was that some cards still have value even today.

"Hey man, thanks for the deal! Appreciate it!"

"WOW, what a steal!"

The players were quick to snap up the deals and paid no attention to the real reason why it was even on sale. It took less than a month to sell almost everything. Some cards remained in my binder; these were important to me. The journey back home after each transaction made me think about these players and them jumping on my cards like scavengers. One can even change it to an "All You Can Eat" international buffet. Impulse and using your emotions instead of logic can lead to your downfall. The permanent damage one can suffer from stuffing their gut with all that food might feel good since most do not think about the long-term effects of excessive consumerism. Speaking of long-term effects, the players who bought my cards do not have the foresight to think of the future - these cards they bought are good now but will they be good five or ten years into the future?

The cards I held on still had value today. My foresight in looking into meta trends of card games and historical trends in real life often mirrored each other. There will always be things (in this case, cards) that will retain their value even ten years later.

My parents had an arrangement after my sister was born that my mother would be a stay home mom. With me coming along shortly after, my mother had her hands full with the both of us. My parents agreed that after my sister turned eighteen, my mother could return to work and return to the industry that she loved. After two long decades away from the F&B (Food and Beverage) industry, she joined Marina Bay Sands as a Cold Kitchen Chef after a friend recommended her to the MBS (Marina Bay Sands) team. It wasn't until my mother left MBS and decided to join her former classmates in SHATEC (A Singaporean Culinary School) at the Singapore Sports Hub F&B team that she realized her potential. The Sports Hub had just gone through a long period of renovation and organizational changes. After a long hiatus of sorting out administrative changes, it finally became operational. With the surge of events organized at the Sports Hub and tons of people forecasted to be in attendance, there was a need for massive hiring to keep up with the demand. The tickets sold out quickly, and there was a demand for food because selling food at a live event goes in tandem with ticket sales.

If you didn't know the profitability of selling food at a live event, you are in for a treat. No such profitable business model ever existed other than selling bubble tea. The amount of markup that one can impose on an item. Organizers can sell a bottle of water for nearly three times the cost of a supermarket. A cup of draft beer costs more than a 750ml bottle of beer. Processed junk food can start from ten dollars for nachos and cheese. Restrictions on "what you can bring in" and the security checks imposed on spectators create an environment where the National Stadium can control what you can consume. A perfect monopoly.

The time my mother started working at the Sports Hub coincided with the long holiday at the end of my high school semester. With card games out of the picture and my wallet starting to look emptier without my father's stimulus, working part-time during the holidays was the best option. The Sports Hub happened to organize multiple domestic and international events that year- talk about stars aligning in my favor. One night as my mother was talking on the phone, she mentioned something on the phone which piqued my interest.

"If you need a job, you can contact me. The Stadium is going to have tons of events. And we are short on staff. If you are interested in working, just let me know."

Like a shark who smells blood in the water, the moment my mother put down the home phone, my body leaped at the opportunity, with the words magically coming out of my mouth.

"National Stadium needs people?"

"Yes, Johann. We need people for our events. There's currently a shortage of hands on deck.."

"I'm interested!" My tone was a little squeaky. It was hard to conceal my excitement.

"Are you serious? Preparing food is not easy. Why not you just do a data entry job or something else?" My mother was concerned about my enthusiasm; she knew deep down the F&B industry was not an easy part-time job to take up.

"Let me please."

After a short moment, my mother took out her phone and called her team to inform them that I was available for work. That's how my first adventure into the F&B industry began. Striving to explore and experience different kinds of challenges has been part of my identity. As a child, I often wondered what my parents did in this industry. Were they cooking all the time? What sort of preparation goes behind the operation? Why are chefs even having meetings? Don't sound shocked at me - Chefs attend meetings to discuss their budgets and what they can prepare with them.

Regulations

Before my adventure in F&B could begin, there was one hurdle. Singapore is one of the strictest countries in the world when it comes to food handling regulations. No surprises there since this country has a reputation to uphold.

The SFA (Singapore Food Agency) exists to regulate the F&B industry. Failure to comply with these food standards would either end in the food business having their licenses suspended, in some cases, revoked. Nothing destroys a business quicker than revoking its license. Certificates are given to food handlers to certify that they are trained in the appropriate guidelines to carry out their duties. Some certificates prove that the candidate is a certified barista, a food safety manager, and a workplace safety manager, just to name a few. Sometimes my mind would drift away and recall some of the countries I've visited. Most of these countries do not have the infrastructure to support and regulate their food industry; this means that the barrier to entry to F&B is much simpler and cheaper compared to Singapore. Any form of regulation makes businesses tougher to operate and is a sign of reckless monetary spending by the government of a country - one key thing that international businesses monitor. There are pros and cons to having regulation.

Before I could start working in the kitchen, I was required to pass a certification. It was called the "Basic Food Hygiene Certification" It was a piece of paper that allowed me to work in a kitchen and do basic food preparations. Taking up this certification was sponsored by the Singapore Sports Hub. A free certification? What a sweet deal. With my mother hounding me to get it as soon as possible, there was no time to second guess or back out of attending the course to attain the certification.

The certification's structure was a lecture with an exam at the end. The certification course took up the entire day, stretching from morning to night. Sometimes I wonder if the certification dragged on so long just to justify the trainer having to work a '9-5' schedule. In my mind, this course was a formality to attain the certification; to give the attendees the same feel as children taking exams. The trainer looked incredibly uninterested in teaching us. Maybe this is the hundredth time he has done so? The job of the trainer has to be soul-crushing. Isn't it?

"I do not believe teachers have any right to give their students life advice."

The above has been a statement that garnered a mixed response from my peers. The idea of a teacher consulting an adolescent is a ridiculous one. Hear me out. These teachers have no experience of what life is like outside of the school system. How could they be the ones to be trusted on such an important topic? With the Asian upbringing in a cosmopolitan city, the usual suspects would be a Doctor, Lawyer, or Engineer. A childhood being conditioned and mapped out by their teachers would strip the child of their own identities; such a shame.

Most parents spend little time with their children, and most public school administrators have become the 'god-parents' of these children. How does the soul-crushing nature of reality that the copy-paste answer of doctor, lawyer, and engineer overrides all dreams they have? The chance to cultivate their unique skillset shattered into pieces with the haunting remarks of their parents. What remains is an empty husk - filled with the echoes of their parent's lamentations. A new generation of machines to replace the existing ones. The centrally planned script will dictate the lives of the next batch of humans - a hive mind seeking its new spare parts.

Working in a job to survive was one of the last things at the back of my mind. That became a big difference between my classmates and me, which led to us never seeing eye to eye. My teachers throughout my public school experience disliked me because of my open disdain for people having no originality. My heart knew that going into something off the beaten path was ideal for me. My teachers didn't like it and tried to bend my will to fit theirs. Now that I look back, there were legitimate concerns about them wanting me to become like my peers. In hindsight, the path least traveled is the most fulfilling. Looking at the industry that Information Technology has become; is proof that my pick for walking this path was an optimal choice.

What happens when the dream imprinted on you becomes a nightmare? Not everyone gets to live the dream forced down their throats in the corporate world. They end up in jobs that serve no end. Most would have lives to work, pay the bills, eventually have a family and then die. It's the sad fate inhabitants of big cities have. Like a ticking timebomb, their lifestyle becomes more and more expensive to upkeep as public spending goes up and up. All it takes is a financial collapse like the 2008 Crash for everything to crash. They spend most of their lives living aimlessly. When one bad day comes, it's all over.

No dream. No goal. Nothing - just a cog in the machine.

That was what my perception of the course trainer was. Did he enjoy spending time teaching people how to handle food well? Was he being compensated well for the time spent being a teacher? How many people remember the type of work he is doing? Years have passed, and the recollection of his face in my memories is gone, let alone his name.

The course finally ended. The certificate was printed and handed to us before dismissal time. The necessary certification required to work in the kitchen was in my hands. Heaving a sigh of relief, I was glad the hurdle was out of the way. Examinations and tests were not my favorite pastime after all. It was time for me to make some dough at my part-time job.

The first event that started the journey was an international soccer match. It was one of the first high-profile events hosted in the newly christened National Stadium. With an influx of international attendees scheduled to attend this event, the Singapore Sports Hub had to ensure its standards were at the highest level possible. My mother asked me to submit my schedule to her for this event. Within a few days, an email arrived. It confirmed my attendance at the event. Talk about urgency. The email gave us instructions and protocols along with how to dress. The type of shoes to be worn, along with the reporting time for the event.

"Woah… you're going to be working at the Stadium? That's damn cool."

My neighbors were surprised to hear that my mother gave me the chance to come and join her to work at the stadium. It was one of the nightly walks we would take to a 24/7 Indian cuisine restaurant to have supper. Having supper was a custom we had every week until we all started to take our diets seriously in our adult years. We spent the whole night talking about the National Stadium. Most of them were more interested in the blue-eyed European beauties that would be showing up for the event as attendees.

The day finally came - event day. The National Stadium was at the Stadium MRT, one of the newest train stations to debut in Singapore's MRT (Mass Rapid Transportation) system. As the escalator brought me up to ground level, it was the first time there were so many people in a new train station.

"Wow…" was the first thing that came out of my mouth instinctively.

It was my first time arriving at the Singapore Sports Hub since its renovation. It was a sight to behold for me as I seldom visited stadiums and played in sports games. There were butterflies in my stomach as my pocket vibrated non-stop. My mother was calling me.

"Where are you? We are about to start our briefing in fifteen minutes!" my mother was talking loudly. It was clear the area she called from was packed.

"I'll be there soon. Just need to navigate around here!" with that, my feet automatically started moving on their own.

Arriving at the National Stadium posed a whole group of problems. The Stadium was huge. On top of that, there were a lot of people in attendance. Queues formed everywhere for them to go through the standard gantry, and there were some VIP queues with private entrances. There was a specific entry for event staff like myself, and my eyes scrambled to figure out where it was. Since the National Stadium had such a complex entry system, finding my way into it took me a long time.

"Hey, I was waiting for you for so long!"

I could feel a familiar voice shouting directly at me from a distance.

It was a family friend of mine, a colleague of my mother's from her time in SHATEC. Let's call him John in this case for confidentiality purposes. It was surreal to see John and even more surprising that he could recognize me. The last time he saw me was more than a decade ago.

"Your mother sent me here to look for you as she's busy briefing her team."

"Hello Uncle John, long time no see."

"Yes, it has been a while." John looked at his watch before continuing. "We don't have that much time. I'm here to tell you the standard operating procedures and the team you are to report to."

"I thought I was supposed to work with my mom?"

"Yes, you were supposed to. Because the admin team thought you were no-showing, they had picked a few other guys to cover for you."

My heart sank as my brain took a moment to process the information. The chance to work alongside my mother was no longer there. Nonetheless, there were shoes to be filled in other departments. John was speaking at the top of his lungs at someone in the distance.

"Eh, James, this boy's name is Johann. Does your team need more personnel? You can have him on your team."

"Eh, what?" before my brain could process what just happened, a towering figure approached me.

"Hello Johann, I don't have time to introduce myself. I'm one of the team leaders for this section. Here's your uniform." James put the uniform in my hands. "Please change into it now. The locker is just behind. See you in two minutes!"

In just five minutes, so much action took place. That was the working world from my perspective. In the school system, you have classes, lectures, labs, tests, and exams. All you have to do is follow the system and not break any glass ceilings. In this world of F&B, it's a whole different ball game. It was a system of organized chaos and adaptability. The people in this room with me are trained and skilled professionals.

When an issue appeared in the school system, the response would take minutes, even hours. Resolving it would take forever. Since there was no urgency in fixing the issue, it was straight finger-pointing. It remained an issue until someone else bit the bullet. It's the culture of having people working jobs they don't like but having to sustain their lifestyles. These public school administrators have no pride or ownership in their roles. Not to say that all of the do, but the black sheep always make teachers look bad. The scene witnessed here was of sheer adaptability combined with the communication they had was something that resonated with me.

If there is a word to describe the structure within the National Stadium, the only word to describe it is "Labyrinth" After changing into my uniform and storing my clothes in the locker, James ushered me into a corner of the reporting area where my teammates were.

"Looks like everyone is here! My name is James, and I am the team leader for this section. Today's event is a soccer match. It is a major event with many foreign delegates and important personnel representing their organizations. Any questions regarding this?" James tried to speak up in the sea of loud voices.

All of us shook our heads. James then continued his speech.

"Great, I am in charge of the overall event for today. The section assigned to us is the bar area. Any of you here have any experience dealing with alcohol before?"

Again, all of us shook our heads. The median age among us all is eighteen years old. James was surprised that most people working part-time at this event were in their teens.

"Amazing… Amazing. We don't have time. Let's go!" James looked at this watch and took out his walkie-talkie as my team rushed towards the lift.

The National Stadium had a design reminiscing of a labyrinth. Some doors you took only opened one way. Some lifts only took you to certain parts of the stadium. Getting lost in the National Stadium was a guarantee without being accompanied by a full-time staff. From the outside looking in, most people would assume that the stadium had a circular design, with the structure of every room revolving around the field. However, it has different compartmentalized rooms with underground levels, staircases that lead to specific sections, lifts that don't go to floors without the keycard, and much more. The design might have come straight out of a cave from a Pokemon game.

Upon exiting the lift, James directed us toward a grand-looking room. It was the most outstanding-looking area in the entire National Stadium because the room had a name. The room was appropriately named: "The Lounge" With the Stadium being strictly brown and gray everywhere, the lounge had a premium feel. It was shiny from the outside, with shades of mahogany and gold.

"No, we are not going in through here. We need to look for the staff entrance."

Taking a detour, James took us toward the entire end of the floor to look for the staff entrance.

"The event is going to start soon, so let me give you a brief rundown on what to expect here" James looked at us with urgency. It was clear he wanted to give us clear and precise instructions. Trying to frame it in a teen-friendly tone was his intention.

"As you can see, there are a lot of guests in The Lounge. Most of the VIPs are in there. We serve alcoholic drinks and snacks in there."

"Here is a tap - this is how you pour the beer from it."

With that, we all watched in awe when James demonstrated pouring the beer from the tap. James held the cup at an angle as the beer poured in. It was a skill that came from decades of experience.

"If the guest wants some foam, is this how you do it."

James then showed us how to operate the machine to produce the foam at the top of the cup.

"This cup is used for drinks. We also have a multi-drink tap if they want soft drinks. And for water, just come to this fridge and give them one bottle of water and a cup." James waved his hands and pointed to them as he told us.

"All you have to do is smile, take the orders, and serve the drinks to them within a minute. Any questions? It is a simple task! I'll see you all later."

James briskly walked away towards the back of The Lounge to the kitchen area to monitor the rest of the event.

In ten minutes, we went to the holding area, to the lift, and now stood inside the lounge. We had a short brief, and now it was showtime. It was the most surreal experience being in an actual lounge with that many guests. The people in the lounge had a different vibe from the type of people you would meet on the streets. As this was a soccer event, the guests were from the host countries and various organizations. The organization that stood out was Barclays. Why Barclays? Growing up, my friends would often talk about soccer. From their conversations, I deduced that Barclays was a soccer team. Years later, I discovered that Barclays was a bank, not a soccer team. Imagine the face palms I received from my neighbors.

It was an intimidating experience for my team since we were all in our teenage years - this kind of crowd was foreign to us. Some of us felt stage fight but quickly shook it off. There wasn't any time to waste as the soccer match was about to start. There would be a torrent of drink orders that these guests would want.

"HELLO! One beer!"

"Can I have a cup of Coke? Thank you so much!"

Within seconds, there was a flurry of exchanges flying around. The orders came one at a time then they picked up speed. There was a visibly long queue in my sight, with the sounds of chatter. I looked to my right and my left; my team was flustered - it was the first time dealing with such a crowd for us. Even though the guests were all extremely courteous and pleasant, watching the queue of quests in front of us was an intimidating sight. The guests looked at us with endearing eyes - I had a hunch they knew we were all juveniles working part-time - something they once did years ago.

After taking a few orders, my team got accustomed to the crowd. I could read from their faces that they were enjoying themselves. The anxiety in their tone changed to the excitement with each order fulfilled. They started laughing and giggling with one another. That's when the long-awaited exchange of introducing ourselves began; something they had forgotten due to the magnitude of the first steps into the Sports Hub. The size of such a stadium could make anyone flustered. As the mood lightened up, a crisis started to brew in the distance.- one brand new type of order we did not fulfil before.

A smartly dressed gentleman approached us with a warm smile. His eyes surveyed the drinks we had. He glanced at the beer tap, then at the soft drinks dispenser, then at the fridge behind where we stood. I could infer from his expression that he found what he wanted.

"Hi, I would like a bottle of wine." The gentleman smiled as he pointed at the wine in the fridge behind us. "Do you mind opening the bottle for me and emptying it into a cup? Thank you very much."

"Open the wine bottle, hmm..." one of my teammates murmured as he gave us a look of despair.

My teammates gave each other a look of shock as we realized that James instructed us on everything - the beer, the water, the soft drinks tap, except for handling the wine. Bottles of wine were something my parents bought and kept in large quantities at home. It was a drink often paired with certain types of food when their friends visited our home for a celebration. The wine was different from the canned drink I consumed. I recalled a metal tool used to open the wine bottle ending with a loud 'pop' sound. What was the name of that metal tool? My brain ran through memories; as though I was executing a Binary Search algorithm in my head. After what seemed to be an hour (seconds in real-time), I managed to find the result - the name of the metal tool.

"Guys, we need to look for the corkscrew opener."

My teammates gave me another confused look as I saw one of them desperately trying to remove the cork with his own hands to open the wine bottle!

"Hold up, hold up! Don't do that. Give me a second, here it is!" my hands reached into my pockets for my phone; a simple google search of a corkscrew opener gave me the results.

As my team huddled around to look at the picture of the corkscrew opener, one of my teammates identified it immediately near the tools area next to the washing area. She sprinted to the corner, grabbing the corkscrew opener. All of us were looking at each other - it was clear we needed one person to take one for the team - to be the one to open the wine bottle with the corkscrew opener. None of us wanted to be the guinea pig to use the corkscrew opener to open the wine bottle. It was as clear as day none of us had ever used the corkscrew opener before.

My heart told me that biting the bullet and doing it was the only option. If not me, then whom? It wasn't the first time the decks stacked against me. Countless times in my life - stepping up was required; being a spectator wasn't something that sat with me. Ownership and accountability go hand in hand; the responsibility of doing my job well was something expected of me. Nobody forced me to take up this job - I could have taken the easy way out and worked a brain-dead data entry job. My mother didn't force me to work; it was all out of my free will to learn something new. Blaming the job was unprofessional since I signed on the dotted line - the responsibility lies on me as an individual. I never understood why people complain about their jobs; if only they approached theirs with my mindset, there would be no complaints.

My hands were shaking as the corkscrew spun slowly into the cork. Fear started to set in. What could go wrong? Is the bottle exploding in my hands? What happens if I mess up and look bad?

"POP!!!"

After what seemed like forever, the cork came out flying and the sound the bottle produced after being removed was a classic sound - a sound that invoked the memories of my parents opening them for their friends. As the bottle was about to be handed over to the guest, James's frame started to appear as he walked briskly toward my team.

"Pour out the wine onto the cup. We are not allowed to give the glass bottle." James tapped me on the shoulder and whispered to me. It was a crucial step I forgot after being overwhelmed with emotions after opening the wine bottle.

With the plastic cup in his hand, the gentleman smiled and walked away as he sipped the wine from his cup. My team then screamed at James for forgetting about teaching us about opening the wine.

"I remembered teaching all of you about opening the wine!" James gave a cheeky smile and tried to feign innocence in front of us. None of us were buying it.

My eyes caught my mother as she was walking toward the lounge area. My heart felt at peace after that nonstop action of beverage action after seeing my mother in living color. Leaving my team behind for a moment, I went ahead to meet my mother.

"How was it, my dear boy?"

"It was tiring; I thought I was supposed to be helping you in the kitchen!"

"Well, plans change. The events team needed someone to fill up the spot at the bar area, hence why you are here in The Lounge."

"I only signed up to work in the kitchen, but this was fine."

"Johann, F&B is not only about the kitchen. There are many aspects of it - this lounge is one of them as well; not everything revolves around food. There is a beverage in F&B. There are also many departments in this F&B team."

Within one event, my perception of this industry changed again. My initial thoughts were that it was all about the food - the planning, the ingredients, the dishes, and the plating. There were way more things about this industry than just one factor. The front house, the backhouse, and the management team work together to make this industry work. This Singapore Sports Hub is an organization; its F&B team is one small part of the system. Many different parties worked together to make this soccer event a success.

Just as my team had time to take a sip of water, a wave of guests entered the lounge. They were headed toward us to get themselves a new round of drinks. My team could not even catch a proper break.

"Guys, it's halftime now. Most of them are here to order their drinks during this period. After this, it should be more slow and smooth. Let's do this together!"

It was as though James recalled the halftime. There was no time to waste; it was time to give our thirsty guests their drinks. My team got to work and fulfilled the orders one by one. That day was an experience of a lifetime - from not knowing how to open a wine bottle - to learning how to pour a cup of draft beer and having first-hand experience working in a lounge. Shortly after halftime ended, it was inching toward the end of the soccer event. From then on, the orders slowed as we noticed the lounge started to have lesser people. Another 45 minutes passed meant the event ended, and the adrenaline which pumped through my veins wore off.

Magically, James appeared when it least mattered and looked at us with a frantic look on his face.

"Everyone listen up. I need all of you to clean up the area and make the lounge area look clean before you guys call it a day." James ordered us and hurried off to the next section.

"Hey, where do you think you are going, James!" John appeared from the kitchen area and screamed at James angrily.

"You have been missing the entire event, running around pretending to do work. What is wrong with you?!" John pointed his finger at James, demanding an answer.

"Wh-what are you saying? I've been busy briefing everyone on what to do." James tried to defend himself. His face gave off a nervous look.

"WHAT! Your role is to be at the lounge with these part-time staff and monitor the situation here, not be a busybody and run around telling people what to do!" John was furious at this point, but upon seeing my team, he tried to remain calm as he noticed we were watching.

John then looked at us and told us what he meant and James's original role. James was the team leader of the lounge section. Despite being in charge of the lounge, he wanted to sneak off to other teams and split his time across them so he could spend his time sparingly and go for frequent breaks during the event. An unprofessional move like this wasn't new to me. There were a lot of leeches in the public school system. Unfortunately, these leeches would grow up and be like James in the real world.

"So the reason you taught us how to pour drinks quickly was so you could run off and leave it to us to handle?" my teammate shouted.

I decided to remain silent and watch the entire exchange unfold.

"No, no. I was going to come back immediately! I had some stuff to settle."

"What? John just said that you are supposed to be stationed here with us to handle the drinks!"

"Ok, I got another meeting now. Thank you all for your hard work today. Have a good night!" Before we could interrogate James, he ran off with another excuse.

That summed up my first experience working in a professional F&B environment. My mother still had some tasks to complete in the kitchen; she told me to go back home on my own before her. A beautiful scene greeted my eyes as my feet took their first step outside. The entire Stadium area lit up with flashing rotating colored lights and the night breeze touched my face. There were groups of people running along with several groups of cyclists having a night cycle. Passing by the National Stadium was part of the journey. Due to the connectivity and small size of Singapore, the entire country has park connectors, connecting various parts of the parks in Singapore. The PCN (Park connector network) allowed Singaporeans to have a "coast to coast" trail from one end of Singapore to another. Several Singaporeans have since attempted it. This group of people was trying to complete it at night. A good choice since the weather was cooling.

Upon reaching home, I took a shower. As the water poured down, the first thought that crossed my mind was to share my experience with my mother and to sign up for as many new opportunities as were available in the Singapore Sports Hub to learn more about the F&B industry.

The next day, I sat down with my mother and told her about the experience and what transpired, me learning new skills, making new friends, and the James incident. My mother listened intently and laughed at the James part.

"He's like that, always running around."

"But isn't that behavior very unprofessional?"

"Not everyone is like your mother, Johann. In the working world, there are a lot of clowns and people who pretend their way out of everything. Not everyone goes to work to 'work.' Some do it because they have no other choice.."

"Really? How do they live with themselves?"

"You will find out over time, just take a break and enjoy your holidays."

My mother's words remained etched upon my soul. I thought people grow up and become better people as they mature. That certainly wasn't the case. Then what do these people strive for in life? Is the end game for them just living like a cog in the machine? One day these people would have children, and this terrible cycle of suffering would be imprinted onto their offspring - cursed to carry on this madness.

"All the world's a stage, and all the men and women merely players." If there is ever a quote that sums up the working world, it probably is that.

CHAPTER 3: THE "FREE" MARKETS

Sometimes, there is a feeling that creeps into my soul that tries to make me look around to see past the illusion that reality is trying to show me. The funny thing about myself is that everyone around me always tells me how aware my consciousness is regarding affairs and how artificial society is. It started as early as in primary school and only became more apparent during secondary school during the various restaurant outings with my classmates. There would be laughter and some good banter. One significant portion would be a 'food coma' induced rant by me after stuffing my face full of food. My mind would go off on a tangent which meant the rants would soon begin.

"Don't you guys think there are just too many restaurants around? We are such a small country, and almost none are fully seated with guests. I wonder how they are even making money."

"Look at the amount of staff and chefs they hire and look at what they are offering on their menu. I'm pretty sure their budget is very tight."

These are some rants that would come out of my mouth when my stomach is full beyond my limits, a food coma setting in to turn off my thought process. My classmates would listen and laugh inorganically, like a bunch of NPCs with no response other than the programmed one. One ear in, another it goes out. It was a tough time finding someone who would resonate with and share the same thoughts as me. Over time as I grew older, my rants would become lesser as the years passed. Even though a part of me wanted to share it, it was best to keep it in my heart and mentally tell myself about it.

The Singapore Sports Hub, where I spent most of my holidays working for, got me wondering how things operated. The budget has to be sky high; it consists of the staff required during each event, the food to prepare beforehand, and the amount of permanent staff handling all the administrative affairs making this business an expensive operation. There are some lull periods where there are no events scheduled for months! Since I started working, my acquaintances suggested we go to the Sports Hub at night for evening runs together. On weekday nights when I'm there for a run, the Sports Hub is eerily silent, without a shred of human existence. The traffic there doesn't warrant a mall to be built there; which real estate developer in their right mind would build a shopping mall where no tenants would want to set up shop? It was clear that the tenants were not earning enough to cover their overhead as the shops often changed tenants every few months.

There's a saying that is close to my heart. It is from the book "The Personal MBA: A World-Class Business Education in a Single Volume" by Josh Kaufman.

"If you're not making money, it's not a business. It's a hobby."

It is one of those quotes that make me think when I think of business ideas. Is it scalable? What is the market share? Does it make money? These are some simple questions I will pen down to evaluate the business case for things I want to pursue. During my teenage years, being able to generate a business case was not my forte. As time passed, along with the luxury of having traveled the world and seeing how profitable some businesses were and why some were not, it became easy for me to pinpoint the ones making money.

The two shopping malls in the Stadium area were not making money. Food offerings there had restaurants that were anything to shout about compared to the various hawkers spread around Singapore in the hawker centers. There needed to be something propelling these malls to remain there because such a high operating budget and prime real estate in such a location would fetch a price. That led to me looking into commercial property rental prices. That one Google search made me realize how doing business in Singapore was no longer an option for a regular Singaporean. It's a price only a corporation with capital can afford. Rental rates per square meter were obscenely high in Singapore; this was seven years ago when I did that search. One can imagine what the rates are today. Singapore is notorious for being one of the most expensive cities to live in - with high residential rentals in the prime districts near the Singapore CBD (Central Business District). There are some tactics that landlords also impose on their tenants. One example is making them sign contracts that lease to them for a year and not every month. This tactic allows the landlords to easily make bank from their tenants with their starry-eyed aspirations of wanting to be an entrepreneur.

Few people count their blessings on how fortunate they are to live in a first-world country. A lower-skilled person working a part-time job in Singapore makes more than a college graduate from other parts of the world. Having been to different parts of the world, the collective state of the world isn't as good as portrayed in the mainstream media. Trips to parts of the world deemed modern and urban are usually not what it seems. On one particular trip to Paris, there was a part of my trip where the train took me to the outskirts of Paris, the scene which greeted me upon exiting the train was one that lives on in my memories forever. The first warning sign was when upon leaving the city center, fewer and fewer people were on board the train. The moment we left the train and navigated ourselves to the stairs to the ground level, the first thing that greeted us was a platform filled with trash and homeless people sleeping on the floors. Graffiti and weird symbols were everywhere. My father asked me if this was the right station as there was a particular shop I wanted to visit.

Upon leaving the station and stepping onto the surface area, an empty street greeted me. The sky was visibly dark even though it was early in the afternoon, and the chill in the air hardened my heart. It was one of those chilling experiences which reminded me of those horror movies I watched on the flight to Paris. There is always a sad, doom, and gloom feeling on every trip to Europe in my life. The shops were open with no patrons. Restaurants were aplenty but had very few people dining in. There were playgrounds on street corners, with no children playing.

Comparing Singapore to other parts of the world, I can understand how appealing Singapore is for people to move here. High wages, security, clean cities, and efficient transport are some of the reasons why. Expatriates and corporate people are attracted to the high salaries offered in Singapore. For the wealthier crowd, the tax bracket is one of those enticing deals which would close the deal for retirees to move here.

A few Singaporeans crossed paths with me and talked about taxes and the different tax brackets; these are few and far between. Until my friend passed me the "Rich Dad Poor Dad" book by Robert Kiyosaki was when my heart knew that there are kindred souls on this planet. Taxes are usually the number one expense people have. Unfortunately, most are unaware of it. It was an eye-opening experience to learn about corporations and businesses having tax reliefs and incentives that led to my understanding of finances and the world of business.

Of course, with more people moving to Singapore for benefits and relocating here to start a new life, all good things eventually end. There was a time in the 2000s when my country was at the peak of its dominance. This peak was enough to gather the interest of our neighbors to leave their nests in pursuit of a better standard of living in Singapore. As more of these foreigners swarmed in like a locust, the identity that built up Singapore was no longer needed. The free markets in Singapore slowly died out, to be replaced by corporations and foreign influence. No matter how much people try to hold on to the identity and history of our nation, the ones in control of our money supply hold the keys to controlling a country.

The hawker culture that Singapore has is the thing that ties Singaporeans to its roots. Once the hawker culture dies out, there isn't anything left of Singapore's history. In the future, our hawker culture will become a case study. Maybe some climate warrior would talk about how unsustainable these hawkers were because they used live produce and didn't use bugs in their food.

The one thing tied to Singapore's identity is our hawker culture. No wonder our hawker culture has been officially added to the Unesco Representative List of the Intangible Cultural Heritage of Humanity. My country's national dish is Chicken Rice which doesn't need any introduction. It's a dish consisting of poached or roasted chicken served on top of a bed of rice cooked in chicken soup, fat, and other spices. The dish is truly out of this world. When I'm abroad and far from home, having chicken rice is something I look forward to once I return home.

Different hawker centers in Singapore are known for some dishes. Some hawker centers are known for only one store; Maxwell Food Center's association with Tian Tian Chicken Rice and Old Airport Road Food Center is known for its Lor Mee. Geylang Serai is known as the place to go for Muslim Cuisine. As a Singaporean, whenever people ask me where to eat, my first response would be to go to one of the top five hawker centers; you would never go wrong. The food offered in our hawker centers is way tastier with a rich history that goes behind it compared to the kind of genetically modified and flavor-enhanced food you find in some of the chain restaurants in shopping malls offered in the 2020 era of Singapore.

So one might ask, what changed? As times passes and more foreigners move into Singapore, the hawker scene that propped up this nation will no longer need to exist. The hawker scene has changed from one where food represents our history to become more progressive. The ones leading the progressive change are the franchise hawker model systems.

These entrepreneurs with business acumen and without culinary experience would easily partner up with aspiring chefs and create a recipe that has rarely had any depth to them. One stall splashed on with the stories concocted by marketing agencies sprinkled with a little bit of SEO (Search Engine Optimization) is an easy enough recipe for a launchpad. Raising capital from banks will be a walk in the park. With extremely low-interest rates (sometimes near 0%), these entrepreneurs can scale their businesses with money that doesn't exist due to fractional reserve banking. The banks would then patiently wait for these businesses to go bust. On the rare occasions that "foodiepreneurs" - as they are called in Singapore by the mainstream media, succeed in their latest food ventures, the bankers would receive their money back.

If you think chain stores by these entrepreneurs are a good idea, don't forget that these stores are for-profit, and there is hardly any passion involved other than making a profit. Some of the products used in their stores often come from questionable sources; who knows what kind of GMO (Genetically Modified Organisms) are in them? There is a reason that my family would only patronize restaurants that either serve Japanese or Italian cuisine. The food served there is fresher and often cooked by a chef with proper training and experience.

However, the whole point of a business is to make a profit while ensuring that the overhead is as low as possible - this scenario is a Catch-22. Operating a Michelin Star Omakase requires fresh and top-notch ingredients. It isn't a scalable business because there is only one chef with that craftsmanship which makes the pricing not friendly to most people. On the other hand, operating a franchise model is a good business model because anyone can pick up the skills required in the SOP (standard operating procedure). Due to the ease of replicating the SOP, it is scalable. The ingredients are cheap but not that fresh. You can't have the best of both worlds unless you're selling chicken or duck rice.

The F&B industry in cities has barely any morals compared to the countries I've visited over the years. Sometimes it seems to me that it is a first-world problem where you have an overpopulated city filled with people. It reminds me of the Mouse Utopia experiment by John B. Calhoun. People living in cities are often grumpy and angry compared to those living on the outskirts of a country. Food served in the countryside is often fresher and tastes better due to the accessibility and the way the product has been grown with the air and environment.

The early days of hawkers and the stories of some of the local chain stores in Singapore often come with the same tone and history. The history of providing food for the laborers building this city from the ground up. These laborers would bring the recipes from their homeland and offer them as a service, becoming the pioneer generation of hawkers. These recipes would change over time, partially due to the availability of produce available, in other cases, due to the diverse background of the pioneer generation and their tastebuds. The hawker culture became a thing of its own as the next generation grew up watching this scene become a mainstay. Modern Day Singapore derived its identity as a nation of "foodies" due to the bustling hawker scene. Only a handful of pioneer hawkers survived due to the next generation picking up the slack from their ancestors and adding the missing piece needed to propel their family's legacy to the next level. Ya-Kun is one brand that has survived the test of time. It is impossible not to have a Ya-Kun franchised stall at every corner. Shopping malls in Singapore have Ya-Kun opening up a franchise there due to the popularity and consistency of their products. Some might say that Ya-Kun is the Starbucks equivalent of Singapore.

The golden age of Singapore's hawker scene is long over. The elderly I conversed with often shared stories of hawker food being at a higher standard in the past. Citing the motivation for being a hawker out of necessity to earn a living in the past compared to the Singaporeans of today who do it to escape their corporate hell - the quality of food is drastically different. It often lacks the taste of love.

Being a hawker is no easy task, long hours and life-altering sicknesses are some effects of being a life-long hawker. My father used to tell me stories about chefs and hawkers who passed away at a young age. The combination of a labor-intensive career and being close to overheated kitchen equipment and their radiation is a deadly combo that is often spoken about, as it remains a taboo subject in the F&B industry. Why would someone spend their lives in a small stuffy unit when they can enjoy the perks of an office job with its medical leave incentives, bonuses, and "stable" wages they receive? Singapore is one of those countries where the benefits of working a full-time job far outweigh the benefits of starting your own food business and shouldering the ownership.

It's amusing to me seeing people talk about the dying hawker culture when the reason for its failure is due to them failing to see the forests for the trees. It is a natural progression of things to come when a country becomes industrialized; you cannot have it both ways.

The more technologically advanced a country becomes, the lesser demand for its history to remain the same. The society would become a bastion for growth and attract foreign capital to it - what is left of the past to build it till that point would no longer be essential for its next step. Hence the hawker culture is being replaced by chain stores that see themselves as businesses and not a culture. One day there will no longer be any hawkers from the pioneer batch of Singaporeans who built it from the ground up. Even if there are, the authenticity is hard to replicate.

When I recall a hawker center that doesn't contain any of these new hawkerpreneur types - one comes to mind - Dunman Food Center; this shows us the number of hawker centers that still retain their roots. One can find hawker stalls operated by first or second-generation owners there.

With the rising rent and cost of ingredients getting higher, with the former being the main reason, many hawkers have chosen to call it a day and enjoy their retirement. The new management who takes over the hawker centers and food courts usually raises the rent by nearly double when they offer a new lease to the existing tenants. Gone are the days when the rental cost less than a tenth of your operating overhead. In today's era, most aspiring hawkers and F&B entrepreneurs can see themselves paying up to a third of their overhead for rent and utilities.

It is sad to see the same chain stores in nearly every food court. The same Chee Cheong Fun, Roast Meats, Fried Rice, and the lot. These stores have no story behind them and serve as just a means to an end for the new generation of hawkers. The owners are never there, meaning that the whole exchange of swapping your currency units for their food is a soulless transaction. The staff working is usually foreigners. These foreigners escaped their homeland in pursuit of better opportunities in Singapore - why would they want to work for a terrible wage back home when they can do the same job in Singapore and earn close to ten times the amount? Their motivations differ from the hawkers who helped build this country from the ground up. These foreigners are here to make that sweet Singaporean dollar. Personalized and tailored service from these foreign stall assistants is an impossible dream. Their mentality is like those from a country where things don't come by easy - a dog-eat-dog world.

Out of every ten businesses, only one will survive of them. "For one business to survive, nine must close" This is the law of supply and demand which remains a hot topic of discussion amongst my business partners. It seems as though this country has a plague of Singaporean's first business venture being something related to food. The idea of a manufactured dream of being an entrepreneur - owning a cafe. I think that real estate owners do have a stake in our public school indoctrination system. These food businesses can range from someone creating the brand new sugar concoction (Bubble Tea, Fruit Shakes), eCommerce sites featuring "premium" foods, hawker stalls, restaurants, and my archnemesis, cafes.

The Cafe Dream scenario

"There are too many damn cafes."

One search on Google for Singapore Cafes, and you will be greeted with new search results every month. There is always some new gladiator in the cafe Colosseum. It is not just limited to the streets of Katong where they are popping up, in the CBD, the prime shopping district in Orchard Road, and several heartland areas where these cafes populate nearly every square foot. It is an opportunistic money grab from urban planners and real estate companies to allocate spaces in their property development to squeeze as much as they can attain by giving it the legal usage as a food outlet by the URA (Urban Redevelopment Authority). The URA in Singapore is the national urban planning authority and a statutory board under the Ministry of National Development of the Government of Singapore. Their role is to designate the use for urban areas.

Before even starting operations, the cafe owner will be staring at the invoice for everything. An investment of six digits is required even before the business starts. The fun does not stop there; there will be the sourcing of ingredients, menu planning, and staff to hire. A runway of six months is an estimate for the cafe owner to know whether their cafe will be a boom or bust. After sourcing the ingredients and planning the menu by copying the most generic cafe food offerings of pancakes, waffles, and something on toast, a cook is hired for the dream to become a reality. The cafe owner knows deep down that this was a mistake. However, there is a chance they can be the one of a hundred who finally end this historical trend of succeeding as a brand new cafe. At this point, the capital expenditure has hit close to one-third to one-half of a million, and will the cafe owner be able to recover everything by the end of six months to justify it all?

The first day of operation begins. Friends and family would be the first few to patronize the cafe. Bouquets with blessings of success at the entrance signify a brand new journey for the cafe owner. Unknowingly to the cafe owner, these family and friends would visit this place out of their familial ties. Unless their products are out of this world, a second visit won't happen. Knowing that the ball must keep on rolling, the cafe owner then engages a few food bloggers and hires a digital marketer to boost the online presence of their cafe. Marketing is required in this era of F&B because most people's taste buds start with their eyes.

The first three months of the cafe would be the best days that it will ever have in its existence. After seeing the burst of customers visiting the cafe during its infancy, the cafe owner would have an inflated sense of happiness - why would they not be? Their cafe might be the cafe that beats everyone else on this battlefield. Only the strong will survive. With this, expansion becomes the next step in the business plan, typical of every first-time F&B owner who aspires to become the next restauranteur like Salt Bae. As time passes and the cafe goes into its second quarter of operations, the cafe owner realizes that business has changed, new customers are coming lesser, and few returning customers have returned. Trying to reassure themselves that it is just a one-time occurrence, they ignore the warning signs and carry on their death march. What is one bad day in the winning gladiator in the cafe Colosseum?

Days turn into weeks. And Weeks turn into months. It has been two months of slow sales, and for the first time since opening the cafe, the cafe owner did the numbers and realized the numbers could not break even. Panic starts to set in as their hopes and dreams start falling apart.

"How could this be? My cafe was doing so well."

The cafe owner's phone started to buzz - it was a brand new message from his WhatsApp group. A good friend has messaged the whole group about a new cafe opening and suggested visiting it. Not wanting to be a wet blanket and missing a chance to flaunt their status as an entrepreneur, the cafe owner willingly said yes to the cafe visit.

"Wow, this cafe looks so minimalistic and zen!" said nearly every friend of the cafe owner as they stepped foot inside the new cafe.

The cafe owner suddenly felt a bit of Deja Vu, the praises, the crowd, and the words used to describe the cafe. There was a team of professional photographers taking pictures of the food. The cafe owner instantly recognized them; it was the team that helped take photos of his cafe's food! With hands outspread, the cafe owner frantically looked for the menu, hoping for the best. To the cafe owner's dismay, the drinks looked the same; the cafe food also looked the same apart from the words used to describe it was a little bit different and featured Hokkaido soft serve with pancakes.

The cafe owner's jaw dropped as the service staff arrived at their table to take their orders.

"Hey, what do you want to order? You are the last one." a friend tapped the cafe owner's shoulder and resumed taking selfies of her caked-up face in the cafe.

The cafe owner recognized the staff as their staff from the cafe! It seems as though the staff is moonlighting. What happened to the text message from the staff that she needed to study for her upcoming exam and couldn't work the weekend shift at the cafe?

The coffee and food arrived, and the group proceeded to take their Instagram pictures to feature on their stories to let the whole world know about it. The day couldn't get any worse for the cafe owner.

Turnover rates of cafes

The above is the kind of thing that happens time and time again. Every cafe owner goes through the same cycle. Even though it was a bit exaggerated, most cafes in Singapore have the same menu and drink offerings.

Every cafe might say that their coffee beans have the best blend and come from the best sources. However, a simple Google search will land you on a few pages of coffee suppliers and the machines they offer - most cafes offer the same drinks; with the same supplied beans at different costs based on their rental and location.

Most cafes do not survive past the one-year mark. Since most sell the same thing, it does not make a difference if you visit Cafe A or B. The market share has been divided too thinly among too many players. And that's also a good thing because if a cafe can survive past the one-year mark, it must be doing something that its competitors are not doing. Once cafe owners start looking at their cafes as a business instead of a passion project, it goes to another level.

One of the cafes which took things to a different level is PS. Cafe. It is a local Singaporean business that started from one branch to more than ten branches in two decades from its inception with two stores abroad; it is possibly the most successful cafe story seen in the Singaporean cafe scene.

What makes a cafe succeed isn't just a story of guts and bravery to take on the risk of opening one. You need a solid business plan, a team, and an experienced chef. Words are not enough to describe how important having a chef is in the F&B industry. Having a chef as a partner can scale things up a notch very quickly. However, chefs aren't that cheap. Often, their expertise can take up a chunk of a business's capital. In my opinion, there are worth it. In the graveyard of F&B, the difference between a food business succeeding depends on the quality of the team. A chef improves the business's chance of success.

What makes an F&B business succeed

A cafe, hawker stall, and restaurant are all businesses. What makes these businesses succeed is the same as a typical brick-and-mortar shop becoming successful. It's also the same as what makes an IT startup succeed. Starting a business without a plan is like participating in a tournament without practice. Planning is just one small part of the business. It provides the blueprint for how it becomes operational. Without a plan to generate sales, there would be no lifeline to carry on the enterprise. Without a plan, there would be no cash flow.

A few months into starting my first business, fate led me to share a table with an enigmatic elder gentleman. This gentleman had a different vibe from the other drunken elderlies chugging their beers and having pointless banter. He dressed in a strap-on, and the bag he was carrying was a brand that was familiar to me - it was a brand not easily accessible and had a floor price above the common brands available domestically. The gentleman spotted me having lunch and joined me at my table. He said how I was enjoying my food reminded him of himself when he was younger.

He started to introduce himself and mentioned that he came from a finance background, having spent the majority of his prime years abroad working in various financial institutions. The gentleman was clearly in his seventies, maybe even early eighties. His sentences were well articulated, and the vocabulary used was those I often read in books from the 1900s. I knew I had to listen to what this gentleman was saying. From stories of his time overseas, he told me not to eat that quickly and to savor every bite of my meal. He then asked me about my profession as the conversation progressed. After telling him about my business, he entered into a solemn demeanor, deep into his thoughts, with his eyes closed.

"Which is more important, your employees or cash flow?" the gentleman asked me upon hearing my profession.

"Employees, without them, the business will not function." it was a quick response from me, confidence beaming out of me.

"Hmm, I understand." the gentleman took a puff of his pipe before continuing.

"Cash flow is more important. If your business isn't generating cash, then you have no employees. No matter how well you treat your staff, they wouldn't work for you if they can't get paid on time. You can treat them as well as you want, but without cash flow from your business, don't expect them to stick around."

Everything clicked in my brain as it processed the nugget of advice from the gentleman sitting across from me. Without any sales or demand for my business offering, there would be no need for employees. I was doing the reverse by hiring employees instead of finding projects for my business. It was a paradigm shift that changed the way I operated my business.

"It is your responsibility to create the cash flow strategy, and then you can hire people for it and expand. That's it. You don't start with the people. You start with the initial cash flow."

That was some solid advice from a random person at the coffee shop. Rarely do people sit beside you and tell you things you need to know. Most of them would sell you courses to relay this information.

"That was some of the best advice ever. May I know what's your name?"

"Hahaha, you don't have to know my name. I'm just a man who happened to be here waiting for his grandchild to finish school."

With that, the gentleman shook my hand and left promptly. It was a much-needed lesson from him. This lesson came out of nowhere; it was as though the stars aligned for us to meet. I have never met this man again after visiting this coffee shop on different occasions.

For an F&B business to succeed, the owner must have a plan. The whole point of an F&B business is the food, with the beverage coming in a close second. Some would say that the drinks are more important than the food for constant revenue coming in during a dining session but based on my experience, the food offering makes people walk through the door and have their butts placed firmly on their seats. Having a chef is required unless you're the one who can cook and have the experience to make it work. The menu is the thing that stands out the most - the biggest reason why most new F&B businesses don't last is that their offering is the same as their next-door one. In my F&B business, my father was the chef that worked with me. My father handled the operation, and I worked on the business side. It was the perfect setting to run an F&B business.

The business side was solely in my control. It started as simple as explaining the menu and upselling the items to my customers. These customers started to return weekly and then daily. They trusted my product and believed every word I said. The products never disappointed them, and they invited their friends to patronize my business. With all that said, that was on the micro-level. The macro-level required a whole new strategy. As my business started to build up, there were certain things I started doing to boost it to the next level - attending networking events, and industry events, and creating an online store. These were some things I began doing to take my business to new heights. Remember that the sole responsibility of a business owner isn't just to generate cash flow from one means. It is to explore and spread the name of your business to other customers beyond your reach to generate even more cash flow.

With most cafes offering the same latte and avocado on toast, there isn't much difference between most of them. You can visit one on a corner in Singapore and order a cup of latte and a week later, order that same cup of latte from another cafe elsewhere. Maybe the cup is hotter at one and not as hot at the other, but you get my point.

Insanity is repeating the same thing and expecting a different result. Over the years, many cafes have propped up, and many have closed down. Aspiring F&B entrepreneurs have done little to no research in their planning stage and jumped into the fire, thinking that their new cafe is the best thing created since sliced bread.

Important business skills.

Unfortunately, the public school system does not teach this skill. Do you expect the school administrators and the teaching staff to care about this? I had to pick up this skill since young when I had to speak with a convincing tone that made me the anthesis of the 'ideal youth' society needs. After starting my own business and several sales pitches I've made to upsell my products, there's nothing more important in business than learning how to sell.

Selling is the same as communicating. Communication makes or breaks an interaction. Coming off too strong will put people off. Coming off as meek will make people think you are insecure. It's only from the experience of talking nonstop that one can become an excellent communicator. The best business people on this planet are excellent talkers. Their speeches and tone can convey the emotions they want their target audience to receive. A capitalist without proper speech patterns and communication skills cannot succeed in their pursuit of liberty; who in the world is buying your sales pitch if you can't communicate?

The art of sales is the pinnacle of communication. Marketing is the art of telling a story. Often when speaking to people younger than me, a common question would surface.

"What career should I pursue after college?"

I would smile at them and respond with all the kindness in my voice.

"Learn how to sell."

You can imagine the look these youngsters would give me. It's a taboo career that their parents always tell them not to pursue. Sales has a reputation associated with the snake oils salesman. I also understand that it isn't as cool as telling your parents that you want to be a lawyer or a doctor. If face value is so important to you, then go ahead and be a doctor or a lawyer. If you don't have a scholarship, then have fun paying off your student loan debt for the next few years of your life. And don't forget the hefty tax one has to pay as a doctor or lawyer. This tax rate is only going higher as we carry on this road to serfdom.

Not everyone can sell - we all know that. But the most significant growth one can see themselves having is always in an area where one is most uncomfortable. Heck, even writing this book is something that is outside of my comfort zone. Writing a book looks easy; what comes next is tougher. There's the editing, the formatting, and the publishing part.

The two traditional career paths that most people can start in sales are being an Insurance agent or a Property agent. Learning how to sell cannot be more important than in these roles. There are some prerequisites for getting your license. Once you have attained the necessary permits, it's time to embark on the most significant learning journey outside the formal education system.

In school, there are often modules that would culminate in a presentation, sort of a sales pitch, where you would be required to present a topic or a group project so that the lecturer can access it and give you a grade. During my time as a student, the presentation day would be the day of reckoning for many. There would be stage fright from my classmates as the baton passed to them to present.

Sales is a part of communication as you are trying to communicate a need for the person to engage in a sales transaction with you. Knowing subtle signs and when the other party is pulling back is very important. Examples of communication are watching people giving speeches and comedy acts; working in a crowd is the highest form of communication that stems from being an excellent communicator. Professional wrestlers are not only skilled in wrestling; their moves are often in sync with how they want the audience to react. Some of the most articulate and confident people I've come across are usually sales related - like a property agent. The ability to communicate is highly underrated. Without sales, your business will not succeed. There is no better environment to learn how to sell than gaining feet-on-the-ground experience by being in a sales role in the infancy of your career.

The other important skill in business is marketing, the art of telling your business's story. Nothing sells more than a brand. What do you think of when you see Nike? It's the swoosh and "Just do it."

How about KFC? It's fried chicken and their famous "Finger Licking Good" Crafting a story for your company is key to making it successful. Tying your business to a brand and crafting campaigns to broadcast your business's offering is a marketing technique used by the biggest companies in the world.

Some people are good at sales, and some are at marketing. It is rare to find the same person who possesses both skills. Marketing in recent years has become an industry employed by businesses looking for the best marketing agency to aid them in launching campaigns to raise awareness for their product.

The rules of education have had a facelift recently as the internet evolved into a platform where you can find anything under the sun. In the days of old, entrepreneurs of the past would have to risk everything on the line without anyone guiding them to build businesses that could stand the test of time. As society and technology progressed, schools and institutions were formed for the next generation to attend. The blue-chip companies became large enough to create goods and services for nations to prosper and created jobs for the masses. These jobs improved the quality of life for the working class. Students from different institutions would graduate and start working in these businesses. The students became the pioneer working class of the nation. A few of these workers eventually leave the company they are working for and set up their enterprises. With knowledge attained over the years of working in a business, the aspiring entrepreneur creates a new business offering a different product or service.

With the above example, how long did it take entrepreneurs in the past to spend time studying, then off to work, and after spending all that time learning from their job to step out and start their own business? It took them nearly twenty years of their life; there is a reason why the average age of a business owner is forty-four years old. Everything has changed today, with the internet stepping forward as the go-to platform for people to learn any skill. Google, Facebook, Youtube, and various websites on the internet have created a whole new industry on its own in the form of education.

YouTube, in particular, has become the platform where education has become pivotal. From a simple platform where people would post videos for fun and laughter, it slowly evolved into a place where content creators would post professionally edited videos. Eventually, institutions and businesses caught on and realized the potential of YouTube. It started a massive snowball as these businesses wanted a slice of this pie. There was no longer a need to raise capital to start a production studio; even though some do, all you need is a camera.

From animal videos to tutorials on doing certain things and travel videos, content creators from all over the world rushed on in and started producing content and uploading it to YouTube. Anyone in the world who has access to the internet can visit YouTube. The information age started immediately as access to information was accessible within seconds. Although a revolution was taking place, there was still a gap in YouTube where videos on entrepreneurship and business were scarce. YouTube, during the early boom, was seen as a platform to find entertainment, with education slowly trailing behind.

During my mandatory National Service in the Air Force, one of my neighbors joined the entrepreneur club in his school. He would spend most of his time talking about entrepreneurship; his goal was to take over his family's business after finishing school. On several occasions, he mentioned a YouTube channel that was blowing up. It was a channel that was talking about entrepreneurship and business. That came as big news as no one has ever branded itself as an entrepreneurship channel; even if it did, how can the team behind the channel make content on such a subject and be entertaining simultaneously?

The channel was called Valuetainment. The YouTube channel, started by Patrick Bet-David, is an Iranian who immigrated to the United States of America when his parents fled Iran as refugees during the Iranian revolution. His family eventually attained U.S. citizenship. An entrepreneur by profession - he started a company based in the financial services industry. After that, he decided to use his experience as an entrepreneur by paying it forward, creating a YouTube channel revolving around entrepreneurship to educate everyone with the purpose of teaching fundamentals of entrepreneurship and personal development while inspiring people to break from limiting beliefs or other constraints. Not only was Valuetainment's content on-point and educational, but it was also incredibly entertaining. There was a time back before the channel hit a million subscribers and there were inching closer and closer to that target each day. When they finally hit the million subscriber mark, I remember being there on my phone when they posted the video.

Valuetainment's success helped pave the way for other forms of content to find a home on YouTube. Economics, finance, and personal finance YouTube channels started popping up. Professionals in the industries mentioned found a new way to monetize their skill sets at a low cost - this kickstarted the new era of YouTube. With this boom of information readily available, people from all across the world could have all the information they needed at their fingertips. YouTube, along with its social media counterparts and informative blogs, became the new golden age of the internet, where it became the 24/7 teacher entrepreneurs needed to get started. The days of attending school, having a career, and then going through the pains of starting a business and learning from your mistakes were an afterthought as various YouTube channels specializing in business content shared their trials and tribulations for the world to see.

Despite this, why are there more businesses failing? The information available was accurate, in theory only. The issue at hand wasn't so much of the information available. The entrepreneur's application of this knowledge remains the deciding factor.

From Employee to Boss

Rarely do people self-actualize and find out why they have failed. From my experience thus far, the number one reason behind success and failure always lies in one person - yourself. You have no one to blame for anything; everything you have in life is a direct consequence of your decisions. The most successful people I've come across have a high degree of ownership instilled in them; without this, it is hard for you to succeed. In business, no one can solve a problem other than yourself.

One key reason for a business's failure always lies in the

entrepreneur. Starting a business is no easy feat; it requires tons of skills. A single entrepreneur rarely possesses all the skills to run a small business during its early days. Businesses are teams, teams of highly skilled professionals working as a team to make the idea become a reality - a properly functioning business with cash flow. What happens if the entrepreneur does have any skills? They just so happen to have saved up a large portion of their money from being an employee and are ready to take the plunge of a lifetime. Money in the hands of a fool is often gone.

Years spent in the corporate world without building a skill to show for is a recipe for disaster. Accumulating money from a job is one thing. Being able to generate cash using a skill without the comfort of your full-time job is another.

As a business owner, market research in one's industry is necessary, usually taking up my free time after my business's operating hours. With the trend of the food industry moving towards a future of synthetic meat, I have started paying attention to the food shortages appearing worldwide. It seems as though having real food is becoming a luxury as the masses have begun accepting synthetic food as a replacement due to these crises. Reading articles and watching YouTube videos would give me the information required, one trend that keeps popping up are professionals in the service and marketing industry leaving to start their own F&B business. With one skill set they possess, they can easily bridge the gap by hiring a marketing agency to fill the areas of expertise they lack.

What happens to the F&B businesses that fail? You rarely hear about them. It is often taboo to talk about the F&B business graveyard. There are many, and often their stories are sad. One can come up with reasons why they fail and manifest before the first day of operation - the entrepreneurs themselves. The leader is the one who steers the ship; they are the one with the direction and the mission for the team. Employees and interns join a company to learn something from the business. If not, why would these people even seek employment and traineeship from a business without a leader?

Being an employee is easy. Stories and complaints from acquaintances over the years would have me squinting my eyes. I wondered how hard taking orders from a boss (who is also an employee), executing them, and then heading home afterward is that hard.

The routine of going to the office, going for a lunch break, and then returning to the office to wait till the knock-off time is the exact description of a job. Some jobs may be different in terms of duration, but in terms of relativity, it's the same. One of the most heartbreaking things about transitioning from being a student to a working adult is the soul-crushing effect of how a full-time career can destroy one's hopes and dreams.

There are two groups of fresh graduates - the first is the "go with the flow" group. This group makes up about ninety percent of most fresh graduates. They are the cookie-cutter bunch we have all seen in our lives, from the classmate, the club member, and the happy-go-lucky guy. Usually, the ones who would dare not branch out of the norms in society, conforming to the herd is the only option for them. These are the groups of students who would huddle together, celebrate, and panic together. From the moment they were born to their first days in school and then to graduation from the education system, they never really had any plans in their mind. With the true going-with-the-flow motion, whichever tide the torrent of change flows, they will just go with it. Exactly how Milton Friedman wrote regarding 'From Cradle to Grave.'

The second group of fresh graduates is the aware ones as they have a purpose in life. This group is the ones we see as leaders in their CCA (co-curricular activities) club, the ace students, the scholar, and so forth. As the true beacon of excellence in Singapore's meritocratic system, society expects big things from them.

However, not all days consist of sunshine and rainbows. This group of excellent people would attain a job deemed a success by society's standards. Due to the harsh realities of society, they would also succumb to the pressure and conform to it, making them no different from the "go with the flow" group. These students would become no different from the 90% of Singaporean graduates. The allure of a female companion they promised to give "a good life" combined with the hefty price tag of a public housing project would render these graduates embracing a path of risk aversion. Why is risk losing their high-paying job in pursuit of becoming an entrepreneur? The devastating effect of working a job begins with spending the best hours of your life in an office. Coupled with being in an echo chamber filled with the overtime work culture can create the sort of effect that can bend even the strongest minds. I have to admit that when I was a full-time employee, being in an environment filled with my colleagues took its toll on my psyche.

The little things of office culture - from the coffee break to the tea break sessions that cost upwards of ten dollars - can create a perfect consumer mindset in any employee. The need to consume more overrides the brain; this slow process conditions the excellent graduates to become motivated with higher wages from a promotion or changing jobs to feed this spending virus of theirs.

From the ashes of despair from the brave souls corrupted by the realities of society, not everyone succumbs to this pit of madness. There is a glimmer of hope in the working force. Some employees are incredibly aware of what they are doing and are maximizing the incentives of working while having a plan for the future. The number one thing that all employees must realize is that their time is finite, while money is infinite. The whole premise of working is to earn a wage, preferably a large one. It may be investing, having a side hustle, or sometimes even setting up businesses to run while having a paycheck from a job. These employees know what they are doing and are intentional with the direction of their lives.

What about the employee who wants to transition from an employee to a boss? Let's say we minus the prerequisites of the employee having capital, the skillset, the business plan, and the guts to do it. There is one thing that the employee needs, and that is the mindset. Before anything begins, the employee has to look at himself in the mirror and ask himself these few questions.

Are they willing to go beyond the forty-hour work week?

Are they prepared to forgo their entitlement to leave and medical leave?

Is it ok to undertake the challenge of having no income for the foreseeable future?

The business has a 99% chance of failure - will you start one knowing that?

Not everyone has a risk tolerance for failing. The education system in Singapore is world-class in giving Singaporeans the foundation for languages, math, and the sciences. However, in pursuit of academic excellence, the lessons learned from failure become an Achilles heel for many. Not many Singaporeans can accept the harsh realities of failing. The education system rewards the most studious Singaporean, not the most enterprising or risk-averse. It's a mind program that conditions the masses to become subservient cogs in the machine, following the system without going beyond their pre-programmed default choice - being rewarded for being a follower is a safer choice than going against the hand that feeds them. Taking the safest play is often the default choice due to our rationality. Trusting our gut and instincts is some pseudo-scientific metaphor for being 'stupid.'

The mere fact is that going without a salary and safety net would dissuade most employees from starting their businesses. God forbid, even if the employee wants to start a business, it is always a cafe. The absolute worst business for anyone to start is an F&B-related business. After my experience of working for my mother at the National Stadium and then going into the field of IT, where the margins are excellent, opening a cafe is the absolute worst thing for anyone to start. Even placing your money into passive investing strategies might work better for the employee than using their own or raising capital to open the hundredth new cafe of the year.

The growing pace and adoption of social media have become a blessing for humanity. In the past, starting a business required a physical location to have a business presence. Now, with various digital platforms and the ever-increasing landscape of the internet with Web 3.0, there are new ways to start businesses without spending too much capital or hiring that many people. The future of work will be online, as seen from the latest, most devastating health crisis that started in 2020. Some savvy employees know of this trend and have businesses leveraging the internet. With the tides of change, some cannot keep up with it. And for those who survive, evolution has taken place.

The Digital Frontier

"Pa, what makes a restaurant good?"

It was a question an innocent child would ask his father. With food revolving around my entire life, I was raised from a young age to know what is good from the trash served by food businesses today.

"The food is the most important, followed by the service. When the food is good, people will come."

My father had the same response. Who can blame him? A chef always believes his cooking is the second coming of Christ.

One of the things that stuck with me was how the previous generation had a different set of beliefs compared to mine. Before my business came into existence, some consultation sessions with my father opened my eyes to the sort of worldview he had. In my father's world, sales and marketing did not exist. The term "salesman" was taboo, as it is associated with insurance and property agents.

After spending time abroad and meeting various chefs, it became customary for me to have the same beliefs my father and the rest of the chefs had regarding their craft. One of the worst things that can happen to a child is to have a limiting belief reinforced onto you from a young age. Little did the chefs know, the world was changing right under their noses. The internet was not only about information. Different industries can also leverage it.

With the rise of the internet, it became a brand new way of advertising. Marketing evolved into digital marketing. The land is limited in reality, whereas digital space is infinite. Building an audience and then channeling it to an advertising hub becomes a trajectory for most digital marketers. From the 1980s to the 2000s, marketing was purely posters, television commercials, and magazines that required subscriptions. It was an era dominated by news agencies with the capital to create advertising campaigns on billboards. The amount to even place a billboard can cost up to a million dollars at a prime location that many businesses could not afford. Word of mouth still is and remains the most reliable way to have a business gain traction.

Hence, I can reason with my father and his peers when they don't believe in sales and marketing. The old-school titans of the food industry still exist. Sales and marketing don't improve the sales volume of these titans. That must mean that a new player in this industry is severely handicapped. So how can a new F&B business keep up with the old-school titans? The digital space can become the launching pad that can take any new business to the literal moon, like Bitcoin (maybe not so much now at the time of writing with the entire Terra Luna fiasco).

Digital marketing is now the end-all-be-all for the F&B industry. If one plans to start an F&B business, you might as well call it a digital marketing company. A social media strategist can go a long way with the right skill set in photography and writing. Online food businesses start from home without a physical location - a smart business move because rental and utilities often take up chunks of the overhead. With a customer base established, the business owner can decide to take it offline.

The initial surge of customers will be good for any new F&B business. What happens if everyone is doing the same thing? How can one survive this war of attrition? Not every food business has a chef with a wealth of experience who can whip up new recipes. Even if the chef can, they are better off working in a Michelin-starred establishment or an airline to receive better compensation for their efforts. The goal of any new F&B business is to become a blue-chip in the location they have set up shop. The only way forward is to endlessly push out content and emails to remind its existing customer base that they are still operating. No matter what, food is the driving force behind this industry and makes or breaks the business. Marketing can be a rocket to the moon but staying in space is another story.

With the healthcare crisis that took place, the future of the food industry looks bleak.

Chapter 4: COVID-19

2019 was the year I graduated from college. Two paths lay in front of me as graduation loomed in the distance. As an undergraduate at the time, I had the entire world ahead of me. Since I picked to study Computer Science as my undergraduate degree, there were a lot of available opportunities. Unlike my coursemates, who were anxious about not finding a job before graduation, I had offers to join various companies. None of these offers enticed me as my goal at the time was completely different - I wanted to push myself to accomplish something I've not done before - to become a multi-card game champion. Winning a championship in one card game was already life-defining. However, winning two titles in two different card games will put me in another category amongst the greats.

The plan was for me to return to professional card games and win another championship before calling it quits forever. Apart from my interest in card games, only reading and writing enriched my soul on that level. Valve, a gaming company famous for being the creators of Dota 2, announced that they were launching a brand new digital card game at The International 2018, Dota 2's World Championship and flagship event. It was a long time since I played cards professionally. And there was an itch to get back into it. A part of me knew that time was running out for the card game industry with the way that Battle Royale and MMORPG (Massively multiplayer online role-playing games) were gaining traction and were going to be the pivotal genres moving forward.

Everything was going as planned until it was not. The digital card game Valve released was called Artifact. The game's launch was dead on arrival. First, there was a paywall where players spent money to access the game, and the cards (in-game items) required more money to unlock. Gameplay-wise, it was complex, which served as a good game for veterans like myself. With the entire player base slowly drying up and leaving to greener pastures in the vast gaming world, Artifact slowly died. For two months, Artifact went from being the most hyped digital card game to the biggest failure in the 2000s. When the events of Artifact took place, it was during November and December of 2018. It was the worst winter for me, coupled with my impending graduation - some things weighed heavily on my mind. Before attending college, my neighbors and I wanted to start a business together. However, all our parents were not very supportive of it and vehemently opposed the idea of a bunch of teenagers starting a business without experience. It seemed every big plan of mine always goes up in smoke and barely materializes to bear its fruits. During the week of Christmas in 2018, my father and I were having dinner. And he asked me what my plans were after graduating from college.

"Johann, what are you going to do after college?"

"The game I'm playing doesn't seem to be working. There is an offer I received from an acquaintance. I'm still thinking about it."

"What's holding you back?"

"I don't like the idea of working for someone. I hate it."

"There is nothing wrong with working. You can work for a while but not forever. The most important thing you need is a hobby and a goal in life. I suggest you try it working first. If you dislike it, you can quit and do something else. Don't make a decision based on an assumption."

That was one of the best pieces of advice my father has given me outside of food.

The Software Engineer's experience

The day finally arrived; it was my first day of work. A few days before officially starting my new job, my mother ecstatically celebrated my next milestone and told me how proud she was of me. I could understand her view; my sister and I have finally grown up and become working adults, an admirable goal for my mother after all that years of nurturing us. The journey to the office put me off. It was going to be an hour of travel from my home. On my first day traveling to the office, I noticed several other passengers standing on the train platforms. It was almost a guarantee that they were also going to work. The scene before me was familiar, and since I'd hit the milestone of becoming a working adult, I could see things more clearly. The dead-pan stares of these adult passengers had come into focus as I stepped foot into the train. Their posture was hunchbacked as they stared into the dark abyss of their smartphones. The years of traveling to and fro the office for them must have taken a toll on their psyche. With that haunting first scene of the office gone, I eventually found myself standing in front of my company's building.

The organization had a building towering over everything else in the distance. The building was the largest in that area and was the largest Information Technology (IT) company in Singapore. After the person assigned to pick me up from the waiting area showed up, she brought me around the different floors to show me what they were doing and the amenities they had. The tour of the office took me around departments and working areas. The first six months of being a Software Engineer went by better than I expected. There were functions and events to attend whenever I had the time outside my regular work schedule. Attending various events in the IT industry made me realize how big of a bubble this all is; how can organizations send their employees to attend events when they are on a payroll? There were close to several thousand people at the time. If you were to add up the total salary divided by the day, it was a loss of productivity that a small business cannot afford to have.

It hit me that my lack of knowledge in finance and business was apparent. Most small businesses could never operate like big organizations with tons of resources. There was more to being an entrepreneur than having the guts to start a business; these big businesses were running at another level. I spent most of my free time after work going through tons of financial-related education.

Receiving my paycheck every month, I was extremely frugal with my spending on things that were not essential for me. One of the big things which changed me was starting to work at a young age at the Singapore Sports Hub. Since my parents cut my allowance from a young age, I had to be resourceful and responsible for myself. Before then, I would often pester my mother to get me this and get me that. Thankfully, my mother would often say ok and get it for me. With the flow of free cash coming in every month with pocket money, there was no need for me to monitor my spending, all the bubble tea in the world was within my grasp. Working a job from a young age taught me the ultimate lesson in life - money is a result of productivity and is hard to make.

Before enlisting in National Service, my bank account had close to five thousand dollars from working part-time, an achievement most youths would not have. Coupled with my extremely health-conscious and careful mindset, I saved close to eighty percent of my National Service allowance and by the age of twenty-two had five digits saved up. Applying the financial education from YouTube, I put my savings to good use and invested in the stock market by DCA (Dollar Cost Averaging) into Index Funds and several other speculative endeavors.

Despite saving and investing everything to make my net worth grow, with a plan to start a business, my colleagues still surrounded me, and their thoughts and emotions did not align with mine. My idea of working and using the capital accumulated to start a business didn't sit well with my colleagues. They wanted to coast at their job and work for the sake of working. The colleagues who joined the organization at the same time as I had all drank the corporate Kool-Aid; corporatism has assimilated them. That is one of the pitfalls that many young graduates make, and that is to take the advice of their senior employees.

One of the best pieces of advice I've gotten was to never take advice from people you wouldn't trade your life with - it is as simple as that. It was clear that most people enjoyed living the herd mentality lifestyle. If you want to know how you will look at the peak of your career's trajectory, look at the seniors in your vicinity.

I watched many youthful and energetic fresh graduates turn into mass-produced robots in months by prioritizing their work over their lives. Some of the banter that my colleagues often make is the need to gain new skill sets in the IT industry, having to switch jobs often to earn more income, and how their bosses are always in the way of them and their perceived outlook on what success is. Everything my colleagues were saying was the total opposite of everything that my financial education was teaching me. They were all living a life where they allowed someone - an employee of a higher rank to control their emotions and livelihoods.

Covid-19 appears

Around the six-month mark of being a software engineer, things started to take a bizarre turn for the worst. Looming in the distance was news of a virus allegedly spreading from a wet market in Wuhan, China. No one was discussing this topic in my topic; most were still in the festive mood of Christmas and preparing for the New Year.

Despite being in total control of my entire financial situation and having the time of my life executing the plan, a part of me was starting to become complacent. I had no goal to achieve during the two-year timeframe I gave myself to be an employee. I spent my time doing social work, going out with other professionals in the IT industry, and attending industry events. With that many social activities planned out, I had no time for solitude. In my youth, time spent in solitude allowed me to rejuvenate and refresh my soul, allowing new ideas to formulate in my mind. Looking back now, I can see how the hive mind worked after leaving my corporate life behind. Singaporeans today are too occupied with artificial constructs, leaving them no time to think and decide for themselves.

It all felt so artificial to me. For nearly two decades of my life, I was either honing my card game skills or building a brand-new project. During the six months of my job, everything that personified the Johann Loke everyone knew was starting to erode and becoming part of the hive mind, just a cog in the machine that powers it.

Chinese New Year came about in 2020, and my relatives came to visit. It was the Chinese New Year celebration that I cannot forget because it was the last time when things as we knew it was about to change forever. My relatives were all discussing this brand new virus that came from China. It now had a name, Coronavirus. It became the talk of the entire evening as my relatives were all speculating about it - no one thought how serious it could potentially be. It might just be like the flu, and it will all go away in days.

Catching the flu during this season where this highly speculative Coronavirus came into the picture was one where the entire spotlight came onto me - it was a combination of bad timing and luck. The general practitioner had to follow a brand new protocol when diagnosing a person with flu symptoms. There was a new protocol to issue "Stay-Home Notices" for patients displaying flu symptoms, a 7-day prison sentence for being sick.

"Are you serious, doctor? I'm required to stay home for seven days?" I asked the doctor with the most skeptical look on my face.

"I have to follow health protocol. There's a chance that you might have the Coronavirus, and we cannot take any chances." the GP informed me with a concerned look. It was the most professionally scripted response I've ever heard.

Me getting the coronavirus? There was no practically zero chance that I could have gotten it, no one exercised and had a better diet than me. The mere thought of contracting coronavirus put me off more than anything else, and it became the focal point of the war in my head. I looked at myself in the mirror and realized this was all nonsense; questioning myself over the insanity of the issue made me look at the man in the mirror, a great hard look at myself.

The greatest thing that the coronavirus did was wake me up from my slumber; how could people accept this situation as it is without questioning the absurdity of a medical prison sentence? The medical system had just issued me an order to be locked up at home, and not complying with it would make me a "public health criminal." Whatever happened to being in control of my own life? I knew that this was the start of some sort of tyranny. Unfortunately, I was the only one in my country who could see past the layers of the brand-new public health bureaucracy about to unfold.

I spent the next week answering phone calls from my colleagues who wanted updates regarding my health to see if I had developed any new symptoms. Several interest groups and sports clubs I'm a part of started to cancel in-person meetups to "curb the spread of the coronavirus." Coincidentally, the world began its descent into chaos with the spread of the coronavirus. The entire continent of Europe started to report on cases of the coronavirus spotted in a few countries.

Immediately, my organization then issued a company-wide email mandating all employees to cancel all non-essential trips abroad. Within a week, the government created a "public health response" team to handle the coronavirus pandemic. At the same time, my organization also instantly reacted by creating its coronavirus response team. My colleagues were stunned by the sudden regulations forced upon them, most of them had vacations planned, and they had to cancel them now. They weren't bothered in the slightest bit about the coronavirus; things were still normal to us. Except the media around us was blaring its horns non-stop on how deadly this virus was. I was livid at how my organization could dictate whether I could travel in "the best interest of the organization." This entire meltdown of events showed me history repeating itself. This "peace" we had for so long conditioned us to lose our guard. I wondered what was next; was my organization going to decide when to go for lunch so everyone won't be close to one another? I sat as a bystander and could only watch the old Singapore turn into a first-world nightmare straight out of a dystopian movie.

My colleagues were surprised to see their air tickets and accommodations refunded to them instantly. Citing the lack of urgency these travel agencies had regarding refunds - the response was bizarrely quick - as though they knew about this coronavirus beforehand. The coronavirus went into overdrive when the United States of America reported its first few cases. When that moment came, the world shifted towards another trajectory. The US is the strongest country in the world at this time of writing, always seen as the proverbial "Big Brother" to every other country - anything the US does will guarantee a ripple effect on everyone else. Lockdowns in certain cities started, and face masks became mandated in the US. With that, other countries followed suit, and eventually Singapore too. April 1st, 2020, was the day the mask mandate and the lockdowns came into existence in Singapore. To this day, I can never forget this day because it was when the Singapore I grew up in officially died. Before April 1st, one of the changes in my life was to cut down on my news consumption. My lifestyle habit became solely books on topics that interest me, email newsletters of sectors, and Reddit, which I use to check on certain hobbies.

The entire notion of every country's news outlet is to sell fear, with the articles often filled with entertainment-styled home affairs which won't affect or make your life any better. The news coverage of international events is biased toward the country's political views, and sometimes I wish that seniors of my country would stop reading them. However, putting on the lenses of a business owner makes me understand why news media are this way - nothing sells more than fear, and business is, after all, business.

With my lack of knowledge of the news and upcoming coronavirus measures, I went for a run and had a security guard screaming at me.

"What's wrong?" I asked the security guard. Don't tell me that going for a run is a problem now.

"SIR, NO EXERCISING, AND PLEASE PUT ON YOUR MASK WHEN YOU LEAVE YOUR HOME!!!" the security guard screamed at me despite standing quite far from me as she flailed her hands at me desperately.

Not wanting to create drama, I took a detour home and spotted a newspaper on the table. The headline read: "LOCKDOWN AND MASK OUTDOORS STARTING FROM TODAY." I remember having to rub my eyes at the absurdity of a front page. I then fired up my computer to check if other countries were in the same boat as mine. Oddly enough, nearly every country implemented the same lockdown and mask mandates. How did such measures get rolled out almost synchronously - like an Apple software update?

Public Health Bureaucracies

The term "Work From Home" started to go mainstream from the day lockdowns took place. Companies all over Singapore began to make their employees work at home in response to the coronavirus. Due to the nature of my industry, my department was not allowed to work from home. While the population was home working, my team was still required to return to the office daily. It became a blessing in disguise to return to the office daily.

The morning commute changed overnight, becoming empty. My trips in the morning to the office would be me alone in one whole carriage. It was surreal to see the entire train platform with one person during the morning peak travel time, and it gave me flashbacks to rural Japan. Upon reaching the office, it was dead silence, and apart from the occasional receptionist, the lobby was empty. My entire department was one of the only ones left in the massive building, and walking along the hallways of it felt empty compared to when I started working and had other colleagues laughing beside me.

The proliferation of coronavirus restrictions began. Dining-in was banned. The nightlight industry imposed rules that were borderline insanity, killing off the clubs and bar scene in one fell swoop. Shopping malls were open, with few people visiting them other than to buy takeaway food. Back then, I didn't think much of the damage the lockdowns could have to the country. The seeds planted were going to sprout into a massive financial crash on a ticking timebomb. My colleagues who usually went out for lunch used this time to head out to buy takeaway food. I usually accompanied them on trips to various hawker stalls, food shops, and restaurants to see the wreckage left behind by the restrictions.

During the early days of the coronavirus, the hawkers weren't affected that much. The restaurants, on the other hand, were devastated by it. The entire business model of a hawker is to sell food as a product. Most patrons before the coronavirus were accustomed to ordering take-out from them. Alternating to a purely take-out model was a seamless transition for these hawkers.

However, for the restaurant, it was not that easy. Their business model is for diners to enjoy their meals and order a few dishes to share. A service charge is chargeable for each dining session to boost sales. With dining not possible, the restaurant has to sell its food for takeaway. That begs the question - who will takeaway restaurant food at such a price without the service and ambiance when they can go to the nearby hawker to get their food? With Singaporeans being incredibly price-sensitive, restaurants had to quickly adapt to the situation and create takeaway bento meals to attract customers.

Imagine paying rental for prime real estate, the cost of all the ingredients in the inventory, and the staff that needs their payroll. The harsh reality of most F&B businesses is that most of them are running on tight margins and have little disposable cash to shelter themselves against any black swan events. With the profit margins being incredibly tight, every single day of sale for them is a make or break. With the Public Health Taskforce's public health bureaucracies, the entire F&B industry got decimated. Restaurants with such a high overhead had to pivot and adapt to create takeaway meal sets, sometimes even offering discount rates for mass orders. Due to the lack of demand for restaurant takeaway food, most of them started to close due to the measures. Those who believed in a brighter tomorrow raised debt to carry on with their operations. A sudden mandate of a no-dining curtailment did more damage to the F&B industry than the coronavirus ever did to Singapore.

When you look at a see-saw, there is an analogy that one can see: "When something goes down, something else will go up." Maslow's hierarchy of needs has physiological needs as the bare minimum for a human, that food is essentially one of the primary needs of a human and ultimately dictates one's behavior. When one can no longer provide optimal living standards for themselves, they have to cut back on certain expenses and luxuries they could once afford. The hawker scene's roots stem from being a place where laborers could get cheap and affordable food. During this period of mass fear and uncertainty, it was a time when it reverted to what it originally was.

Hawker food is Singapore's national treasure. To some, it is an institution where they dine every week. To most of the working crowd, it is a source of cheap, fresh, and tasty food for their meals. In Singapore's short history, hawker food has been the go-to food for most Singaporeans. Sometime along the way, the coronavirus became designated the term Covid-19. Coronavirus will now be called Covid (for clarity purposes). The Covid measures and mandates somehow made the hawker scene vibrant and rejuvenated. Queues for certain hawkers were longer than usual. Some of the hawkers who were not as popular suddenly saw their sales bump up to the skies and had long queues for the first time.

A carrot cake stall that I frequent and whose owner I know told me that the queue for his stall starts at 7 am and doesn't end until he closes at noon. His patrons would just stare at him as he fried the carrot cake. Despite the queue extending to the toilet, it did not deter people from ordering from him. I even asked my colleagues why they did not buy any takeaway food from the restaurants they enjoyed eating in - the answer given to me was the same reasoning as I had - they only dined there for the ambiance. It took one black swan event for everyone to reach down to their hierarchy of needs and settle for the simple option.

As the hawkers started seeing their best days again, the restaurants and cafes were all shedding blood and tears. Throughout this period, many restaurants and cafes decided to call it quits. The Covid measures and mandates, coupled with the future of Covid being certain, were some reasons for the closure of many F&B businesses. Some of them decided to downsize and become hawkers. Entrepreneurs from other industries spotting the trend of hawkers being a "pandemic-proof" business, decided to venture into the F&B industry. These same groups of entrepreneurs became hawkerpreneurs, opening chain stores everywhere.

The Health, Wellness & Fitness industry was also equally damaged, with in-person fitness sessions, curtailed due to "health & safety" reasons.

Remember the see-saw analogy earlier - when something goes

down, something else goes up? YouTube changed education, and digital marketing changed the way marketing was in the past with social media, emails, and websites. Technology advances, and with Covid measures and mandates enforced worldwide, there were now certain technologies and platforms created pre-Covid, which were ready to swallow everyone as a whole.

With the technological adoption of online meeting platforms, Zoom became the main star of this adoption. With the in-person meeting restricted to less than five people and social distancing measures implemented everywhere, it became a hassle for people to attend meetings. Imagine talking with your mask on and having the person sitting far across from you. Companies started to adopt Zoom and Microsoft Teams for their virtual meetings, and WFH and remote work slowly started materializing and becoming more commonplace.

Another sector impacted was the trade shows and events space. For months, businesses that relied on organizing events in real life had zero revenue. Savvy entrepreneurs who knew that going online could become the default moving forward started to dabble in online meeting platforms and saw the potential of hosting online events and seminars.

Gradually with each month that passes and the end of Covid-19 nowhere in sight, and with cases starting to rise on an upward trajectory, some people would naturally become more paranoid of one another. Add on a mask and social distancing to the mix, and we have a case of massive paranoia and psychosis. Looking at Maslow's hierarchy of needs and knowing that food is part of the bare minimum to survive, what happens when you need food and are not willing to risk your "health and safety" to be exposed to some bad actor who is sneezing? That's when people started defaulting to food delivery apps; in Singapore, these apps are Grab, FoodPanda, and Deliveroo. Food delivery platforms have a reputation, not often a good one; its price point was not worth it for many, and people before Covid would still enjoy going out in a group and having a meal. Why would I order overpriced food when I can walk to the town center and buy it myself? Of course, you would, unless you are incredibly paranoid about something like a virus.

The Gig Economy

Singapore is not known for being a country being cyclist-friendly. Despite the Singaporean Government's best intentions to create one, in the form of the Park Connector system. Riding bicycles didn't go mainstream until expatriates started flocking here in the late 1990s. When the bicycle riding trend started, it became a polarizing topic.

Expats started to ride on the roads with bicycles, and in some cases, they were in huge groups as they cycled in unison from one point to another. My father was a cycling fanatic, having imported bicycles from the USA and being one of the few people who only ride Cannondale mountain bicycles. He doesn't ride in groups because of the stupidity of being in a group wearing those ridiculously overpriced cycling gear, and if one guy decides to slow down, it would mean everyone has to.

With the roads and pavements of Singapore not equipped with the infrastructure to become a cyclist-friendly country, the day when cycling takes over would become the day when Singapore officially starts going down the drain, and it did. With Covid-19 looming in the background and being the focal point of discussion everywhere, food delivery platforms that did not see the light of day suddenly had the spotlight on them. People who feared for their lives and did not want to spend even a fraction of their lives outdoors started to use these platforms to order their food. These apps started seeing their demand go up. These platforms decided it was time to double up, realizing they needed to enlist the help of restaurants and hawkers. They needed a plan - it was time to disguise themselves as the proverbial wolf in sheep's clothing.

"Your business is failing, and you need a digital platform. Let me help you out by listing it on my app! Of course, there is a catch to it."

Restaurants and newly opened F&B establishments that decided to brave the storm by opening and operating during Covid-19 defined a new era of bravery. With their sales plummeting to record lows and barely having any food traffic to start, they desperately needed a messiah to save them. The messiah soon arrived in the form of the holy trio - Grabfood, Foodpanda, and Deliveroo. Enticing them with carefully crafted emails on how they can boost their digital presence to the moon and aid them in gaining traction for their takeaway sales, these F&B establishments signed a deal with them and enlisted their help. There was not much of a decision to be made, the business was on the verge of collapsing, and when help arrives, you jolly well take it.

With the advent of F&B establishments starting to digitalize and having their offerings available online, eating anything you crave is as easy as whipping out your phone and tapping on anything your heart desires. Except there was a catch, the wolf needs a cut of it too! Dishes priced at a relatively affordable price now cost up to one-third more than usual. The increase in cost is to pay the food delivery app a cut on "helping you out."

With the upward growth trajectory of the food delivery apps and the volume of orders, there was still a missing piece that needed to fit the jigsaw puzzle - can you guess what it is?

There was a time while serving National Service when my neighbor would often talk about entrepreneurship and was involved with his school's "Youth Entrepreneur" club. During some events, he would invite me along with him. Seeing all these new startups created often gave me a weird outlook on this startup ecosystem. Isn't it all just creating a digital platform?

The ones involved with the materials - from exploration, discovery, mining, refining, and then having people from other parts of the world handle the nitty-gritty work that most people would turn a blind eye to ultimately produces it. The digital platforms were simply a middleman aiming to "disrupt" the industry in their mission statement. There was no production, no labor, no nothing. Just a Charlatan, promising to use his app's algorithmic superpowers to process the information on his platform that could change the world.

So tell me, who is going to do the work? The founders need to sell the vision and raise funding. The engineers need to chug overpriced Lattes and "hack" their way to creating the MVP (minimum viable product) to meet the founder's whims and impending fundraising deadline. Who needs to do the heavy lifting to fulfill the transaction? Are the founders going to pack the stuff ordered? Are the founders going to head underground to mine the materials? Of course not - they are just the middleman. The missing piece in this "disruption" economy is none other than the manual labor aspect.

The framing and tone of marketing used were excellent. These food delivery companies spent more on marketing than on their engineering teams.

With headlines such as: "Be your boss today!" it wasn't surprising to see many young folks jumping on the bandwagon and becoming their boss. Before this surge, food delivery apps such as Grab was commonly associated with the private transportation hire app. Years ago, Grab also did the same promotion to have more people sign up as their taxi drivers by putting out headlines as they did this time around for the food deliveryman campaign. With Grab, Foodpanda, and Deliveroo going into overdrive to mass-hire manual laborers to meet the never-ending amount of orders on their apps, the true pandemic - the pandemic of cyclists in Singapore was about to begin.

Chaos on the streets

At the end of 2020, Singapore started to ease its public health bureaucracy to allow its population to dine in again. Mass events were now allowed to take place. The country was treading on thin ice, attempting to lessen restrictions while maintaining the infection rate. One of the issues cited by the Singaporean Government was the lack of healthcare resources, hence the reason for some of the more extreme measures. F&B businesses were still trying to recover from the two-month no dine-in and only takeaway measure during the early stages of Covid. However, with the social distancing of one meter required and the limit of dining per party restricted, the dining in spaces of F&B establishments was cut by half.

Throughout the two months of no dining in, food delivery apps started to pick up volume slowly but surely. The easing of restrictions did not slow down the food delivery app's growth trajectory because most people were still WFH and not required to go to the office. I remember going out for a run near the end of 2020 and seeing more cyclists. I thought that the population was attempting to keep fit. Within seconds, there was horning and shouting from the cyclists, instantly puzzling me. A simple glance at the back of their seats and there it was - a delivery pouch attached to their backseats. Articles and commentary by the mainstream media soon followed suit on the rise of food delivery sighted everywhere.

With 2021 and the "delta variant" coming around, a new wave of restrictions came in with new variants, and the cases escalated to all-time highs in Singapore. Singaporeans thought that the initial mandates were a one-and-done thing. That Covid would just end, and then they would just live their lives like it was before Covid. But this time, with the massive fear pumped into every media outlet, people embraced it more willingly. Like a Shepherd leading the sheep, everyone around me started to believe in the madness of Covid. The first time the restrictions came, it was a dry run. Now with the new measures, it was the real deal. Food Delivery apps started to go into overdrive with this new wave of restrictions. During 2020 it was the test run - there was adoption but not anything that important. In 2021, with the new public health bureaucracies, food delivery apps became the hottest thing on the market. Companies have adapted and started to digitalize their workflows with more remote working tools like Zoom and Docusign meant that with new restrictions, they were ready to initiate WFH policies on the fly.

With that one announcement by the Covid taskforce mandating the new public health restrictions, companies started to allow WFH permanently without returning to the office. Food delivery apps became boosted by companies offering meal allowances by partnering with companies for their WFH employees, and with that, the complete assimilation of the herd was complete.

There was also another group of deliverymen that sparked controversy - it was the PMD (Personal mobility device) group. PMD is the devices such as the electronic scooter, bikes, hoverboards, etc. Before bicycles became the norm for food deliverers, many used PMD as their primary vehicle. The PMD is an easy, no-effort way of delivering food - hence many people picked it up. Unhealthy and obese people signed up as food deliverymen because it was an easy way for them to make money while not breaking a sweat. The speed and ease of using one made adopting it seamlessly easy.

With the streets of Singapore filled with bicycles and PMD, it became an awful sight to see. Many people enjoy the ease of ordering their food via an app - scroll click - that's it. The consensus is - "since there is no dining in, everyone should be at home, right?" that's the most shallow thinking I've heard. There are people on the streets, but not everyone is at home working. The majority of people are still around. The deliveryman, wanting to earn as much as they can from their orders, often fulfilling multiple orders simultaneously, blitzing through the narrow streets to fulfill them.

What could go wrong? Everyone should be WFH; the entire nation is WFH. If only life is that simple. Most people have been desensitized to reality and believe that their office job is a real job when they are nothing more than paper pushers and glorified administrative assistants. As food delivery became more popular, the risk of accidents from it increased as well. How can such a thing happen? It's simple. The more desensitized a society becomes, the higher the rate of tragedy.

Morality during trying times

I am an avid reader of books. During the highs of the Covid-19 restrictions, I bought more books and read more than usual. One of the things apart from finance that caught my attention was history. Not the kind of watered-down history that our respective education system teaches us, the history that one can learn from to ensure that the same mistakes do not happen again. Most of society's problems stem from them not learning from the past. Humanity is more concerned with modern distractions, while inflation from a fiat-based monetary system destroys their lives.

Black swan events seem random. The kind of events that pop out of nowhere and change the trajectory of the world is moving in. Covid-19 seemed like a Black swan event until one was to dig deeper - I highly suggest looking up Event 201. For the longest time, what is deemed bizarre and "impossible to happen" doesn't seem that random if one digs deep enough.

The Gulag Archipelago, written by Alexander Solzhenitsyn, remains one of the most damning books ever written. One particular chapter talked about morality and how humans can go to such extreme and barbarous lengths to exact punishment on others opened my eyes to what happens when a nation descends into chaos. When the entire era of the USSR (and the Gulags) ended, the author stated that the Gulag's administrators all turned a blind eye to what they committed during the horrors of the regime.

Stating they shouldn't be held accountable for it; they weren't to be blamed for it as they were doing their jobs! Blame the law! Blame everyone else but not me - I'm innocent!

"Don't blame me for hogging the streets of this country; I need a job to pay the bills!": says every food delivery rider. Restrictions to Covid-19 destroyed industries - the workforce globally decimated, leaving many stuck at home without a job.

The whole purpose of a job is to get paid based on the labor put in - that's it. Whatever a company tries to sell you is just pie-in-the-sky NLP (neuro-linguistic programming) to convince you to sign up for it. Many workers had their jobs taken from them and were in the darkest recesses of their minds. Without a job, there wouldn't be food on the table. Without an income, their lives were in disarray. With barely any savings in their bank accounts and being one paycheck away from being broke, it was a desperate time for those affected by the Covid restrictions. The initial wave of food delivery riders started from the no-dining restrictions and had a substantial sign-up rate. The second wave of food delivery rider sign-ups took this entire gig economy into overdrive. Many people who got their jobs taken away dabbled from industry to industry but couldn't find a fitting. Some were unemployed, lacking the skills to switch from one industry to another. Becoming a food deliveryman for many unemployed people became the best option available. It was a simple job - with a bicycle and a smartphone as its barrier to entry. With that demand for takeaway food and WFH, becoming a food deliveryman was the best option for the time being. Besides, this group of people can finally become their boss too!

"To hell with the streets not being equipped with the right

infrastructure! I'm going to hustle and make my money, and that's all I care about!"

The above was the mentality of the food delivery riders everywhere. Unlike Covid, the food delivery pandemic was visible. The streets started becoming congested with these food delivery riders; it was a period when pavements became unsafe. Do you think these food delivery riders care? Of course, they do not; when a society becomes fearful, its morality depletes in tandem with it.

Only when times are good; does the population virtue signal about caring about one another.

The goal was to make money in these chaotic times of uncertainty. Doing whatever it takes, disrupting people on pavements, on the roads, and even in neighborhoods - it doesn't matter to them. A combination of PMD occupying the pavements and bicycles zooming on a hybrid of any path they can take became the scene of any street in Singapore. I am fortunate to live in a zip code where there are barely any food deliverymen who come, but whenever I make a trip to the heartlands, there will always be one who rings their bell from my back to tell me that they are here to greet me!

Every action has consequences, and the risk of accidents from food delivery rose. The elderly and some youths lost their lives due to the reckless actions of these food delivery riders. It was a dire time for families who had to live with Covid and then have their loved ones taken from them because of the lack of morality of these desperate black sheep.

Even though the Singaporean Government issued a ban on PMD a year before Covid-19 started, cyclists and motorcyclists still fulfilled the orders. I had conversations with a few F&B business owners regarding food delivery; trying not to reveal my position and stance on food delivery, I became the person asking the questions and dictating the flow of the conversation. Unsurprisingly, most F&B business owners still condemn the government's PMD ban! Citing the loss of revenue for their businesses, they hated the decision. The capitalists of old would be rolling in their graves when they know the psyche of this generation's capitalists. The lack of empathy in pursuit of profits never ends well.

The Gig economy at its height

With the food deliveryman pandemic a part of our new lives in the new normal, the rise of the gig economy was underway. With office jobs becoming WFH by default, there was a new gap required to be filled by the low-skilled workers who lost their jobs in sectors such as tourism. "Wealth is never lost; it just changed hands." this is a famous quote used by investors and entrepreneurs who discuss market crashes and how money flows from one sector to another. The money flowed into the healthcare sector, with the masses begging for a vaccine to protect them. Soon after, the healthcare sector started to massively push for research and studies on Covid-19 to create a vaccine; whoever could create one quickly would be able to capitalize on the market demand and make significant profits.

With social distancing in place and the need to enforce the public health bureaucracy on the populace, 'Stool Pigeons' was introduced to the nation by the Covid taskforce. The role of the Stool Pigeons was to walk around key areas in Singapore, such as shopping malls, nature parks, and places where groups of people would be out together in public, and to ensure that social distancing was practiced between distancing between groups. Think about the absurdity of this job (is it even a job that the free market needs?): the whole world is in chaos, the placement of human capital into a sector that doesn't generate goods and services for everyone but is, in reality, curbing the production of it by enforcing social distancing, how is this even an economically viable job? Quoting a famous economist Peter Schiff - "Good Government Policies equal bad economics." he was spot on with that.

The Stool Pigeons became the talk of the town. Picture this - it is a beautiful weekend morning; you wake up early in the morning and put on a pair of overpriced running shoes to go for a run at your nearby park. The first ten minutes of the run were exhilarating. With the wind in your face giving you the tailwind to push you forward, the start of your weekend can never be better. After finishing your run, you look for a water fountain to quench your thirst. Suddenly from the corner of your eyes, you notice a dash of red, not just one, but two. The Stool Pigeons are here. In true Stool Pigeons fashion, it was a fat old lady together with a male who thinks with this bright red shirt; he is a true hero of the nation. With the words "STOOL PIGEONS" (the real words cannot be named) proudly emblazoned on the backs of their shirts and the health of society as their core mission and purpose in their hearts, the proud duo reminiscent of Jessie & James from Team Rocket are ready to unleash their holier than thou powers on YOU, the poor runner!

"WHERE IS YOUR MASK? PUT IT ON IF YOU ARE NOT EXERCISING!" the Stool Pigeons screamed at you.

"I just finished exercising, and I'm sipping water." you tried to reason with the Stool Pigeons. You know that reasoning is futile; these Stool Pigeons command the power of public health with absolute might.

"PLEASE PUT ON YOUR MASK AFTER DRINKING. WE ALL HAVE TO PLAY OUR PART TOGETHER TO FIGHT COVID-19!!!" With that the Stool Pigeons duo stopped tormenting you and whipped out their phone, there was going to be a Pokemon Go raid coming soon, and they can't afford to miss it.

That, my readers, is how the Stool Pigeons function. In a park, when one is enjoying a nice walk, the heroes in red will appear behind you and tell you to put on a mask because you aren't exercising.

Do you enjoy having a hike on a nature trail? Don't worry. A group of friendly Stool Pigeons will be waiting for you in the corner to dictate you put on a mask and practice social distancing!

How about window shopping in a shopping mall? Our Stool Pigeons will be walking with you too. They need to ensure that patrons practice social distancing from one another. One of the craziest things that some Stool Pigeons were notorious for ensuring social distancing was the measuring tape fiasco. What is it about, you may wonder, let me enlighten you!

Imagine dining in a nice restaurant. The friendly staff has already implemented social distancing and hand sanitizers everywhere. With tables distanced accordingly, no guests were allowed to intermingle between different tables (I know it sounds absurd).

Managers doubled down on ensuring their staff obeyed the public health bureaucracies. As the night went on and the patrons soaked in the ambiance, with a lack of music playing (No music was allowed so that the guests would not stay on too long after eating, one of the measures introduced). From a distance, the heroes in red appeared, and the Stool Pigeons appeared after a long night of window shopping, and they wanted a slice of the pie of this establishment. Like a celebrity, they needed no reservation and could speak to the restaurant manager like their own boss. The Covid task force has given the Stool Pigeons the almighty powers of a health god, and the restaurant cannot refuse entry to these stool pigeons.

The Stool Pigeons invited themselves into the restaurant; all floor staff stood at attention. The Stool Pigeons patrolled the dining area to ensure everyone was safe from Covid-19 by keeping their distance from one another. The service manager knew what the Stool Pigeons were up to and quickly whipped out her mobile phone, dropping an emergency message to the restaurant WhatsApp group to inform the kitchen staff that the Stool Pigeons were there!

The kitchen staff received the message, went into overdrive, and started adjusting their face masks properly. Imagine working in a fiery hot kitchen with tons of equipment emitting heat and an overwhelming amount of orders - putting on a face mask was the last thing on their minds as it was almost impossible to breathe in the kitchen!

Let alone the kitchen staff have not left the kitchen since they started their shift - what sense does it make to put on a mask when they are not in contact with anyone else other than themselves for hours? Logic does not apply in times of fear and uncertainty. The Stool Pigeons slammed the kitchen door open. With their hands behind their backs, the Stool Pigeons pranced around the kitchen with a skeptical look. Their heroic deed concluded to ensure the restaurant staff was safe from Covid-19. They had a small huddle session and decided to carry on their heroic acts elsewhere.

From out of nowhere, the Stool Pigeons spotted an anomaly from a distance! There were two tables incredibly close to each other! Like a vulture spotting its prey, the Stool Pigeons flew in opportunistically - it was time to strike! The service manager gasped as the floor staff looked in horror, realizing their mistake. From the sling bag with neverending content like the Wardrobe from the Chronicles of Narnia, the Stool Pigeons took out the ultimate weapon of choice: the despair device, the weapon of destruction, their justice hammer - it was the measuring tape! Using the measuring tape (of justice), the Stool Pigeons measured the distance between both tables, and they fell short of the Covid-19 restrictions guidelines of one meter! The patrons having their meals disliked the Stool Pigeons having the time of their lives tormenting their dining experience; imagine spending hundreds of dollars on a date and having these Stool Pigeons spoiling it. The Stool Pigeons whipped out their phone, which was strangely on the Pokemon Go screen when unlocked, and snapped a picture of the health crime committed by the restaurant. Raising their head to the ceiling and flicking their wrist, the Stool Pigeons signaled the service manager to come over. The Stool Pigeons informed the service manager of the health crime the restaurant committed - how could they be such crooks not making sure that the patron's health was not safe from Covid-19 by sitting one meter apart? With a crime committed, the Stool Pigeons were to report this incident to their higher-ups (if the Stool Pigeons were this high up in authority, who else could be higher up than them on the hierarchy, god?).

One of the Stool Pigeons then whispered into the ear of the other. There was another pressing matter that required to be solved by them. With that, the Stool Pigeons took down the restaurant's address and the key staff to contact. They had a new issue to resolve - there was going to be a five-star Pokemon Go raid to attend.

The "New" Economy

The typical part-time job was working in an F&B establishment or being a retail staff. The Covid-19 restrictions made part-time workers lose their jobs and look for new jobs to make the dough. At the same time, countries globally started implementing a health passport for contact tracing: it was an app designed to "check in." If anyone who checks in has Covid, it will notify people in the same place as the person who has it to go into quarantine immediately - not doing so would become a punishable offense by law with the new Covid-19 laws passed based in different countries.

You might be thinking - there is an app being created worldwide for Covid-19; maybe different countries have different apps, but how does that create a job? When you leave money that is not earned but given to people who don't know how hard it is to make it, the misappropriation of funds happens. As a result, the Warden Pigeons - a brand new job, was created.

We have Stool Pigeons acting as the quasi-health police, so what do the Warden Pigeons do? The Warden Pigeons' task is to sit at a table at the entrances of venues; be it shopping malls or key indoor venues like gyms, and check on people's check-in status. Yes, that's it, a job where you pay someone to sit and check on the image of a screen. Austrian economists and entrepreneurs would be screaming over their heads right now.

Displaced part-time job workers flocked in to take up these roles. Even during the days before the Covid-19 restrictions, most low-skilled workers weren't as keen on joining the F&B sector, but with this easy-to-do job and authority bestowed upon them as front-line heroes during these trying times, it was not a tough decision for them to take! No such time in history has such money-making opportunities existed. Part-time jobs in the past paid peanuts and were physically demanding, but now all you have to do is do barely any work while consuming neverending mindless content on video streaming platforms. How great can life be?

Society changes forever

Gradually as living with the Covid-19 restrictions became more ingrained into our society, the hive mind assimilated the population into the new normal. Contact tracing became normalized with a smartphone always in the hands of the user. The social distancing between parties was automatic; people would sit far away to avoid one another.

In restaurants, with the one-meter distancing enforced, diners would angrily look at the other table because what happens if the damned fool has Covid-19 - that fool can spread it to them! Mass paranoia was at its peak, and it took two years to transform our society into a new one. The change that made the most impact was mandatory mask-wearing. If there was one measure that did more than the rest, that was it. The ability to look at a person's face to read their emotions is pivotal in developing bonds; the notion of bonding and getting to know someone from the facial expressions they give out. The power of smiling can have tremendous effects on the human psyche. The day the mask-wearing became mandated was the day emotions died. Suddenly, without being able to look someone in the face to tell what's on their mind is gone, it has become a guessing game as to whether the other party wants to talk to you or not. People started to converse and look at each other less. The mere fact that talking with a mask on makes the person feel bad also played a part in it all; the suffocating effect of talking and breathing with limited oxygen was a terrifying experience.

I can only imagine the youths born in this era and the ones living through it. Online classes were rare during my time - they happened only annually as part of the school curriculum.

There was a rare time when a volunteering event took place one year into the Covid-19 restrictions period. It was a beach clean-up session. After the beach clean-up session ended and on the way back home, I took the bus with a fellow volunteer. My fellow volunteer was a junior college student, and she was talking about how the school has changed since Covid-19 started. Before Covid-19 restrictions began, her school would have various events and sports carnivals. Students would have the time of their lives, playing sports competitions and participating in them. When the restrictions started, the school became just a place to study. Eating in canteens with classmates was prohibited, and after class, the school would become empty - the entire school would just be a place for attending classes. Classes online took place at least once a month during this time. She hoped schools would return to the fun days before the restrictions started, and as she told her experience, I sat there and listened intently, thinking: "Will we ever go back to the days before March 2020?".

As we arrived at the town center from the beach, she asked me if I wanted to have lunch together. I already had planned on meeting a friend for lunch, and I remember her forcing a smile; I knew she was disappointed and sad. Thinking back, I should have had lunch with her; it has probably been a long time since she has socialized with someone since Covid-19 started, and having a meal during these times of uncertainty would have made her day.

The Vaccines arrive

In 2021, the first Covid-19 vaccines were ready for the masses. Countries all over the world, with their citizens tired of the Covid-19 restrictions, started to beg for the vaccines; it was a whole year of having their lives disrupted, and all they wanted was for things to return to normal.

Singapore started its national vaccine program to have the entire country's citizens inoculated. Most of the population went for the vaccine to protect themselves from being infected by Covid-19. As soon as the vaccination program started, some of the people who took the vaccine reported side effects, citing feeling ill from taking it, and in some cases, a handful of people died from it.

As the vaccination program started, the cases of Covid-19 spiked, and the Covid taskforce decided to introduce even more restrictions to curb the rising infection rate. The Covid task force introduced Vaccination-Differentiated Safe Management Measures (VDS, for short).

Naturally, some people would choose not to take the vaccine, citing the safety and speed of its creation. The people who decided not to take the vaccine had their liberties taken away. This VDS created a divide in Singapore among the vaccinated, who believed that if everyone were to take the vaccine, the country would be safe from Covid-19 and return to normal. And the unvaccinated who did not want to take the vaccine.

Both sides blamed each other for their choices. The VDS started with the unvaccinated unable to dine in public, and then it rolled to them getting banned from entering malls and public recreation facilities. And finally, the last straw which broke the camel's back - no vaccination means not being able to return to the office, with some companies firing those who did not take the vaccine.

Globally, the same thing was happening. Many people weren't sitting well with the decisions made by their respective governments. Civil unrest and protests took place against the measures as people globally no longer saw themselves as divided but united against a common cause. One which could snowball out of control if they were to lose it once - freedom and liberty. I was well aware of these protests against the VDS measures, even from Singapore, a country known to only feature news that is deemed appropriate for the masses to consume.

The whole world was against the VDS except for Singapore, and somehow the reason why would shock most people. It isn't because Singaporeans are afraid of the government. Neither is it about them being Kiasu. The reason? Singapore's history. Our modern history. Modern Singapore is barely sixty years old. We have only half a century of history to tell.

Despite our short history of existence, modern Singapore has only a history of success under a benevolent government. With our country built on the backs of incredibly hardworking Singaporeans under the leadership of our charismatic founding father, Lee Kuan Yew, modern Singapore has become the wonderful country it is.

Creating the best domestic and international policies, Singapore became incredibly enticing for aspiring entrepreneurs and people worldwide to leave their homes for greener pastures. In the 1980s, Singapore became the most prosperous country in Southeast Asia. Compared to the rest of the countries in Southeast Asia, Singapore had a reputation as the anomaly in a region that wasn't known for being advanced.

Malaysia was on the precipice of becoming one. Vietnam, Cambodia, Indonesia, the Philippines, and Thailand weren't mainly known as "first world countries" during that period. With this background laid out, Singapore is only in its first century, and we haven't had a history of having crazy dictators. With success after success that Singapore has achieved in its short history, coupled with praise from the foreign diplomats, we as Singaporeans have a national identity of being responsible citizens to the rest of the world. I would be surprised to visit a foreign country and introduce myself to them. Upon hearing that I was from Singapore, they would be in awe and immediately respect me and my country - that is how the rest of the world views Singapore.

The rise of Stay-At-Home Companies

When the WHO (World Health Organization) announced that Covid-19 was a worldwide pandemic, the financial markets went into a doozy. It became the crash in the markets that defined my life thus far. Despite knowing that the 2008 financial crisis was much worse, the Covid-19 financial crisis took place during a period when I was more aware of the circumstances. Having experienced the biggest crash in my life and seeing my colleagues panicking over their investments losing a lot of value, I was incredibly calm about the situation. Having played card games professionally for so long paid a dividend as I watched my investment portfolio drop by nearly 20-30%, maintaining a poker face and contemplating my next move.

I started observing various industries getting whipped and forced to close, but the IT industry I'm in was showing incredible resilience to all of this. One of the biggest strengths of an IT company is that everything is online, and with an internet connection, virtually working from any location on this planet is a reality. The rise of remote work and the demand for online tools became a hot commodity. Despite social media dominating as an entertainment and advertising tool, the use of these social media platforms has yet to show its true strength.

At the time, only a handful of IT/Tech companies stood at the forefront of this shift - Facebook, Google, Apple, Amazon, Microsoft, Oracle, and Adobe, to name a few. The financial market crash made the stock evaluations of these companies relatively cheaper to purchase. With this foresight, I decided to double down on my investments. Another sector I was looking at was healthcare, a vaccine was going to be the most significant thing to pay attention to, and I also entered a few positions in that industry. With my big bets on healthcare and tech, I knew that the next step the world would take was one where Big Tech would engulf everyone as a whole.

Slowly but surely, work from home (WFH) became the default as Covid-19 started to pick up and cases in Singapore started to increase, making the bewildered herd panic and beg the government to impose more measures to keep them safe. Remote work, which in the past wasn't readily available, became more common, and more tech companies started to offer it as the default option for their workers and new hires.

Due to some odd occurrence, a year before Covid-19, Google Hangouts was the tool often used by my community work group. The idea of traveling an hour to meet in person didn't seem time-conducive. I suggested using Google Hangouts as I often wondered what else Google offered apart from the search engine. To my surprise, Google Hangouts functioned better than expected. Apart from a few minor hiccups, it was a smooth application that solved major problems for my group. The only problem with Google Hangouts a year ago before Covid-19 was that mass adoption of online meetings would be a problem - a catastrophic change needed to happen for people to change their habits. At this point, they should just call me Nostradamus.

Singapore is a victim of its success. Its prosperity and growth as a nation, being achieved faster than any other country nearby, has led to the population believing that the ones in charge of creating the policies are always right. With each new Covid-19 restriction implemented, the population agrees and complies wholeheartedly.

With no history of going through a civil war and the horrors of a power-crazed emperor, as seen in previous dynasties, Singaporeans today have no idea what it is like to live through strife and chaos.

Countries like the US and Russia have been through so much in recent memory. Their descendants were the living and breathing embodiment of their past. The US went through several central banks in the past to learn the horrors of a central-banking system but ironically has one today in the form of the Federal Reserve System (the FED). Russia had gone through the USSR era, where the entire country fell into a worker's paradise, with communism taking root in this country. The devastation of central planning by the soviet government led to countless lives being destroyed and sent to work in the harsh tundras in the Gulag system. Several European countries, with their monarch's rule of tyranny in the past, made them forever untrusting and skeptical of their governments. Due to the Singaporean government's track record of never failing its people, the population has grown to adopt this mantra of the "government is always right." Hence, there was little to no opposition to the extremes of the VDS.

If one were to dig deeper and understand the psyche of a typical Singaporean, it would be of a city-dweller, combining first-world living standards with those of a third-world population from Asia. It is essentially the embodiment of everything Aldous Huxley in his dystopian fiction novel 'Brave New World' is. A society where its citizens are eternally happy, following the rules and just doing their job. Every citizen lives in eternal bliss to uphold the status quo, not opposing anything set out by their central planners; any opposition to the rules results in their exile of them to another part of the world.

After fifty years of upward growth, Singapore has become the embodiment of success in the world. Singaporeans and expatriates choose to live here despite the strict measures that the country has - especially the notorious chewing gum law where it is banned to chew one with fines imposed.

It has become common to live with the rules and accept them. Would you rather live in a third-world shithole fearing for your life every day despite living in a mansion, or live in Singapore with rather forgettable rules and live in eternal utopia, just like in Brave New World? Even for myself, I decided to live in Singapore despite everything. The reason why? I've been to many parts of the world and seen the ridiculous state countries have become. Doing a cost-benefit analysis in my head, I would always pick living in Singapore over any country in the world (maybe spending some of my time across other countries too). Singaporeans love to complain about the state this country is in, but it always stems from their comfort and security of living here and having no outside experience of the harsh realities of this world. The grass isn't always greener on the other side.

The great reset brought a new world order to the fray, and the entire world changed again. There were talks about a "Fourth Industrial Revolution" that is taking place, which utilizes artificial intelligence (AI), certainly already developed in the shadows.

And this begs the question: "How is it going to end?" From the various useless jobs created to maintain the Covid-19 restrictions, the systematic decimation of the real economy - forcing people to social distance and stay home instead of working, and the rise of WFH tools, there is a line in the sand that is going to be touched. Central banks globally have been printing money nonstop to stimulate the economy together with the impending CBDC (Central Bank Digital Currency), which will become a reality in a few years.

The metaverse is the digital world where the next generation would be emersed without leaving their homes, seemingly the next frontier. Plans are being developed and planned for the next decade. Before unveiling what I think the world will become, let's take a trip down another path - one which we will carry on from where we left off - My experience owning an F&B business and what led to it during the worst market conditions.

Chapter 5: Running a Business in a Crisis

It was a whole year since Covid-19 appeared seemingly overnight and changed the world as we know it. It also meant that it was almost the two-year mark of me being a salaried employee comfortably living a cushy life. Taking the train to the office, then heading back home, and occasionally going out for dinners with my colleagues and friends have become a routine in my life.

It was the type of life that many people would want; all you got to do was do some work, decide where to have lunch, and then head home after that (maybe with the occasional overtime work). Throughout my entire time working as a Software Engineer, my experience was nothing but amazing, being surrounded by a motivated team. There were tons of perks to being one, with the main one being the respect automatically given to me because being a software engineer was the hottest commodity in the market due to Singapore's push for the nation to have more of us.

It is a big problem, reverberating to every part of our society because we often do things that make us look good despite not enjoying any part of it - everything we do has become just for show, at face value. We have a social media culture where showcasing the best moments of our lives to the world has engulfed us and played a part in this. It felt good telling everyone that I was a Software Engineer, but I knew the time was up. There was a path that awaited my return.

At the end of 2019, I attended an appreciation ceremony for volunteers at Sentosa. It was a fun-filled day with food, drinks, and a trip to Universal Studios Singapore (USS). Having visited every Universal Studio in the world, it was going to be my first time going to one in my own country. I was accompanied by a friend from my community service group as we split off from them to explore the USS together. We took some slow-paced rides together and overall had a great time. There were many times abroad I would be alone in theme parks, exploring it all on my own from dawn to dusk. It was the first time I explored a theme park with another person who was not family. During our time throughout the night, there was one question she asked that I can remember till now.

"Do you enjoy your work?"

Despite enjoying "life" as a socially accepted role as a Software Engineer, a feeling of sadness engulfed my soul; there was more that I wanted to accomplish. A meaningless career of being in IT for more than a decade wasn't something I wanted to pursue.

Many people don't enjoy their work. They simply work for money to put food on the table. Maybe some people do, but that's a rare anomaly. Before I started working, my father and I had a discussion where he gave me a two-year timeframe to go to work and then make a decision after. Two years quickly flew by, and the time limit as a Software Engineer reached its expiry date.

The empty office

I was not the only one about to reach the two-year mark of being an employee. My colleagues, who started around the same time as me, had also reached this milestone. One practice that has become commonplace in the corporate world is the idea of "jumping." A practice where a person jumps from one company to another to earn a higher salary after a set amount of years, two years being a good enough length.

Unlike the other departments, the team I started with was still the same, and nobody had left yet. Every other department had WFH policies in place except ours. That might be why my team remained intact even though many have jumped ships. When an employee is WFH, do people think they are working? No! They use this time to stream TV shows or search the internet for a better job elsewhere. News of employees leaving for greener pastures started to flood the office, and the topic of discussion was often the high turnover rate.

As I embarked on my journey as an entrepreneur, I learned from a young age that retaining an employee has always been the biggest issue. My neighbors who own businesses always cite that retaining talent is the number one issue they face. A big competitor in the form of a massive MNC (Multinational corporation) can easily poach their employees with a big pay raise and better benefits. The difference in the capital that a big organization has compared to an SME (Small & medium-sized enterprise) is like night and day. A big organization can easily hire any amount of prospects with their neverending budget, often subsidized by whichever country they are in, with the government pumping in money for them. An SME would try to minimize their hiring while ensuring that every single employee is tasked with various roles to maximize the cost. Listening to and watching colleagues around me starting to leave for better prospects further justified my friend's woes, and from both sides, I can understand their points of view.

Eventually, the plague of "jumping" reached my department. One fine morning, one colleague not too far from me walked across the office, approached the senior engineer, and gave him a letter. It was a letter of resignation. News quickly spread during the week. An emergency meeting happened, where all the key staff from my department were involved. Within the next few weeks, the office became emptier as more people started to tender their resignations and clear their annual leave days. It became such a big problem that each staff attended a one-on-one "catch-up" session with their direct manager to air their grievances.

Eventually, my turn came to meet my manager. I had a resignation letter with me, one that I wrote on the same day I started working, except the date was empty. Every venture in my life has a start and an end date. This time around, my time as a Software Engineer has come to an end.

Chef Simon Loke

My father, Chef Simon Loke, is a man who is not known to sit idly around and let time pass him. At 62, with a four-decade-long career in culinary arts, the F&B, and the airline industry, he retired with many accolades and accomplishments. Upon retirement, he spent his time going for long walks and hikes around Singapore. Even before retiring, he spent his weekends cycling for hours and bringing his motorbikes to the jungles in Singapore to perform stunts.

From this part on, I will refer to my father as Chef Simon for clarity's sake.

Now that his weekend activities have become part of his original working hours during the weekdays with his retirement, he was incredibly restless. He decided to un-retire as he had too much free time. Within a day, an associate recommended him to become a development chef for a brand new F&B business involving Fish & Chips.

Not wanting to spend his days idle any longer, he jumped on the opportunity and got to work. It took him two months to get sick and tired of retirement. Within a few months of him providing his expertise in the Fish & Chips business, it became a success and had many stores popping up everywhere around the island. That business name is "Big Fish Small Fish."

After a year at "Big Fish Small Fish" has made the business successful with his magical touch, Chef Simon immediately got bored again. He wanted a new challenge. As a Chef, deep-fried food was something he didn't particularly enjoy.

To this day, he is the only man who removes the skin and fat of a meat dish and then consumes it. Chef Simon made sure my dietary habits were healthy, and some quotes he mentioned about food have become my mantra which I share with others.

The first one: *"If you don't recognize the words on a label, don't buy it."*

This quote relates to the mass-produced foods available in supermarkets, from milk and packaged processed foods. Going to the supermarket to get a packet of almond milk often leads to a rabbit hole of google searching, where 90% of the components involved in making a packet of almond milk are alien to me. This revelation led to me buying baked almonds and then using a slow juicer to make cold-pressed almond milk for my consumption; no doubt it doesn't taste as good as the packet one, but it is something that I made myself, giving me the confidence to consume it. One upside of buying mass-produced items is the longer shelf life if kept in the appropriate storage, whereas the downside is only not knowing what was in the process of making them.

The second one: *"Know the source of your food."*

I have only seen Chef Simon eating food prepared by a chef he trusts or cooked himself. The source where you get the meat is so important that it affects how it tastes and the preparation methods. There's a big reason fish and chips always use lower quality fish, and steamed fish require fresh fish. Fish and chips are all about using lower-quality fish because of the batter and oil, and when deep frying will mask the taste of the fish. Cooking Steamed fish, on the other hand, requires fresh fish to bring out the flavor of the fish with a bit of seasoning.

The scary thing about the food industry is the use of genetically modified meats, like chicken, where the size of it is just big; just look at that monster-sized chicken leg sold in supermarkets. The biggest news to hit the shores of Singapore is the ban on fresh chicken exports from Malaysia. It led to a massive outcry from the masses that the conflict between Russia & Ukraine was responsible for it. Singapore's national dish is Chicken Rice. Fresh chicken is the main reason for the dish's authenticity. With the ban on chicken exports, the entire country went into an outroar. "What will happen to chicken rice?" Many chicken rice shops were on the brink of pivoting to selling another item for the time being. Some shops were on the cusp of closing down for good.

The option of using GMO frozen chicken was not even an option by the chicken rice shop owners as the frozen chicken will make it taste like a dish served in a "Kitchen Nightmare" episode. Our local hawkers have ethics regarding the food compared to the rest of the food industry, who would feed you GMO chicken for a profit. So the next time you dine in a minimalistic-looking cafe, look at the menu and see a chicken leg dish, kindly ask the staff what type of chicken it is.

And the final one I'll share: *"Desserts only taste good because they're sweet."*

Chef Simon has always been known for his desserts. From making traditional kueh to cakes and pastries, there is a myriad of desserts he can make. One caveat when making his desserts he would share with me is the quote above. Unfortunately, desserts aren't the only type of food that falls into this category; drinks like bubble tea and carbonated soft drinks also fall prey to it. Without the sugar component in those drinks, it'll just be water. Fancy drinks in aesthetically looking cups with added sugars summarize the bubble tea craze.

Speaking of desserts, the one common factor in them is the sugar component. There aren't many people who can enjoy a plain croissant on its own. Speaking of desserts, the cost of a cake from an online store can start from 9 dollars a slice. Nine dollars for a cake is as good as buying lunch and dinner from a hawker center. The price of desserts has gone through the roof, with these dessert chefs popping out everywhere after a short stint in some random restaurant, enabled by the digital marketing agencies which paint them as the second coming of Jesus Christ. So remember, the next time someone tells you how good a dessert tastes, just imagine it without the sugar. You'll probably thank me for saving your wallet.

The Social Enterprise

You can only imagine the kind of precision and thought that goes behind every dish that Chef Simon has created in his career, combined with the moral compass he has to serve food that not only tastes good but is also nutritional. Around the time I started my career in Software Engineering, Chef Simon joined his friend's venture, which was a social enterprise - his friend needed a breath of fresh air into their food offerings.

The thing about social enterprises is that they are businesses with a social impact. It doesn't function the same way a private enterprise functions, where it is for profit to meet a market's demand. A social enterprise is a different business where it serves the community. The social enterprise required some help, and Chef Simon's friend reached out to him for his expertise. Before Chef Simon joined the social enterprise, my mother helped in it for a while. My mother cited that working in F&B was already hard, and adding on the additional pressure of handling the special-needs staff was another ball game. However, before my mother left the social enterprise, a thought came to her head, "How nice it would be to own a restaurant of this size one day." Funny how things turn out in the end with the mere thought of a suggestion.

Chef Simon always loves a challenge and decided to join the social enterprise to turn it profitable. Within a month of his joining, he introduced a lot of new dishes and became the missing link required to take the social enterprise to the next level. With a social enterprise with a good mission statement combined with a product that was something to shout about, the restaurant became very popular, and things started to look good for it until it all came crashing down when the biggest boogieman of the decade reared its ugly head - Covid-19.

With the Covid-19 public health bureaucracies introduced, the restaurant saw its worst month in sales ever. However, they were quick to bounce back and experimented with various takeaway sales methods. They avoided using the food delivery platforms as the markup imposed by these platforms made the price astronomically expensive for the consumer. As the airline industry was massively hit and since many aircrews were grounded, the social enterprise started to have a few aircrews come and work in the restaurant.

When the public health bureaucracies eased up, the restaurant resumed its rise with the bad days behind them. However, there was one big problem the restaurant had, the labor cost. Labor cost will always be the heaviest expense in an F&B business, with many savvy F&B entrepreneurs minimizing the amount of labor required per shift to make them multitask various roles into one. Food businesses that fail often attribute their failures to the amount of staff standing around playing on their phones and chit-chatting. Even though the restaurant was making a lot of revenue, it was bleeding from the inside with the amount of staff they had, from the grounded aircrew, the existing service staff, the special needs staff, and Chef Simon himself.

Flashy entrepreneurs chase revenue, and savvy entrepreneurs chase profits. As Robert Kiyosaki says: "It doesn't matter how much money you make; it's how much money you keep."

The second dine-in ban

A business that doesn't keep track of its numbers is doomed to fail. It doesn't matter if you make a million dollars every month in sales when you are spending a million and one dollars to make it. During the entire existence of the social enterprise, Jane (Chef Simon's friend who owns the restaurant) is very involved in attending seminars and events to promote its cause.

Jane is rarely involved with the daily operations of her business. Due to the nature of a social enterprise, raising private capital and taking money out of your pocket is not required. Donations from corporations and handouts from the government are common ways social enterprises raise their funds. Covid-19, having decimated several industries, reduced the donations coming in as the businesses donating were not making as much as before. The restaurant was operating with money from external donations and its sales - for as long as another black swan event didn't happen, all should be good.

As we all know, the black swan event happened again. The second dine-in ban took place in May 2021. With the brand new public health bureaucracies, sales dropped nearly 60%. With the public being acclimatized a year ago with the first dine-in ban and reeling from the shock of the Covid-19 cases being at an all-time high from the paranoia everywhere, the fear and uncertainty kicked in, and there was chaos in the minds of the masses.

With WFH policies being prepared and practiced a year ago, the

WFH immediately kicked in as default. As the restaurant was in a university compound, every staff member in the university began to WFH. The university's public health measures made the restaurant lose every customer it had, and even the takeaway sales were affected due to the low traffic. Jane and Chef Simon did the first business recovery plan by reducing the number of staff, but it still was enough. Next, they tried various outreach methods and takeaway sales plans. None of these strategies worked.

It was an ugly period in this restaurant's history, and the time has come to declare the business insolvent. The donation money was running dry, and the sales could not break even. If the business had a bit of capital accumulated from being savvy with the labor during the good days, they would have enough cash flow to survive the down periods as the Covid-19 measures wouldn't last forever.

Chef Simon has been waiting for this day for a long time. Since he joined the social enterprise, he has dreamed of having this restaurant - coincidentally, like my mother.

The Golden Path

During the meeting with my manager, I handed him the resignation letter (except the date was changed, only the template remained the same). Since joining the organization, I've always mentioned that working as a Software Engineer was a chapter of my life - being employed in one sector was temporary and just an experience. Perhaps I would return to being an employee in a different industry one day. Who knows?

Many would say sharing your goals and true thoughts with your managers is a bad idea, but I digress. Most people are upset and miserable because they refuse to be true to themselves. They live miserable lives due to bottling up their true thoughts and not turning their dreams into reality. You don't need to be asleep to live the dream; you need a plan and to stick to it. My manager then dropped the corporate act and started talking to me like a friend. He wished me the best in my future endeavors and was happy that I got it all figured out. And so, at 26 years old, I officially retired from working as a Software Engineer.

News quickly spread in the organization, and several department heads and key appointment holders heard of the news of my leaving. There were plans in my organization to have me move overseas for exposure, and there were shocked by my decision. They assumed that my leaving was due to heading to greener pastures. Upon hearing from my manager that I was going to start my own business, they were all in awe at my decision. Nobody in the organization had left at such a young age to embark on their journey.

I wasn't going to open an F&B business; the initial plan was for me to start a media-related business. I started a podcast during the Covid-19 period, and it was finally monetizable; the plan was for me to go all-in with podcasting and content creation - pivoting from the current content I was producing in card games and switching to another. I was also going to commit all my time to finally becoming a professional digital card game player for a short period of my life to win the world championship.

Funny how things never go according to plan. While I was having dinner with Chef Simon, he mentioned how the social enterprise was falling apart; the sales were not hitting the target amount, and funding was running dry. He was excited that it was finally time to launch the takeover plan and become the new owner. The social enterprise had three outlets, and his idea was to take over the restaurant as he had already built up the clientele there.

Chef Simon wanted to own one more food business before returning to another round of retirement. His first food business was a hawker stall he opened three decades ago with my uncles. Upon finishing the menu and recipe planning, he left the business as he had an opportunity to go to China, which was developing in the 1990s, to be a chef in their new hotel. His goal was to resume his entrepreneurship journey and call it a day.

With each passing day, Jane's hope of sustaining this restaurant diminished. Labor was at the bare minimum to lower the operating cost. Food wastage was at an all-time high due to abysmal sales. Finally, on June 2022, Jane gave in to all the surmounting pressure on her and agreed to hand over the restaurant to Chef Simon. At a favorable takeover cost on top of that.

Chef Simon told me the good news and asked if I wanted to take over the restaurant with him. There were a few mixed feelings on my part; I had a media business I wanted to pursue for the longest time. Starting a restaurant during this time was a bad idea; food businesses were going out of business. I had been holding on to my savings and investments since I was 18 years old, and taking it out to gamble on a restaurant didn't seem like a good idea. There were better business ventures to pursue.

On the other hand, I've always wanted to own a food business; with my parents being chefs and most of the people I grew up around being my father's colleagues, it was inevitable for me to start one. I knew one day I would be starting my restaurant with my associates as a venture; I didn't know that day would come so soon. However, owning a food business was only a temporary affair to check off in my long list of business ventures. My interest has always been in creating stuff - writing this book was the natural progression from having a blog to recording & producing a podcast on my own.

The exact thing always happens before I plan on starting something. Every time I plan a new venture, it doesn't happen, and it always ends up being something else. It took me a few days to think things through. Since the Covid-19 measures were in place, it was possibly the worst time to start a food business. Knowing that the changing tides of small enterprises being decimated worldwide with corporations taking over was happening, I decided to start this food business and get it out of my system. What's the worst that can happen?

With an end date in mind, Chef Simon and I agreed to work together in taking over the restaurant, and after meeting with Jane to discuss the takeover process, it was official. On 31st July 2021, my first food business was born.

The Chaotic Start

"When it rains, you find the nearest shelter and wait it out."

It was the week before the official takeover of the restaurant and the final week of my serving my resignation notice. Funny how it's called "serving" as though it's a prison sentence.

I was out clearing my leave and went out for a morning cycle. The route I took was the same every weekday, with weekends being an alternate one. My cycling route would take me from East Coast Park to the world-famous Marina Bay Sands. Most tourists would recognize MBS (Marina Bay Sands) as a hotel with a ship (or a big oval) at the top housing the infinity pool. If you enjoy visiting scantily-clad IG influencers, there should be a picture of them there when they visit Singapore for "business." We all know what they mean when they say they're entrepreneurs.

This cycling routine came about when my department started to practice WFH. Since I no longer had to go to the office in the morning, I had time to myself. WFH doesn't work. Even the whole idea of working in the office is flawed. Most of your work can be settled in four hours or less, depending on the sector. WFH is great; imagine having three-hour lunch breaks during your office days and barely any work to now being stuck at home with any work to do. There you have it - why Netflix stock soared so much during the WFH and remote work era.

On one particular day on my usual weekday route, a massive rain came out of nowhere. My first thought was to turn around and head home. The second thought was to seek shelter and wait for the rain to stop. I went for the final option - to cycle in this massive rain. I wondered what made me carry on riding in the rain - was it because I was finally a free man? Most people would head home, especially if they have a remote meeting later in the morning or they need to submit a piece of work. I had neither of that - I was finally living life on my terms; it was the best feeling in the world. The rain had a magical effect on me. Until National Service, I never enjoyed exercising in wet weather until I went to one. In that instant, all fear and doubt about starting a food business dissipated. I knew that sometime in the future, my preconceived thoughts about entrepreneurship would radically change. My food business wasn't just any business I went in with no knowledge of - I have Chef Simon as my partner, possibly the best chef in the world.

Starting a business usually requires more than just a plan. From that date, we got verbal approval from Jane to take over the restaurant - our starting operations were a short span of two weeks. Imagine how hectic the schedule was going to be. Initially, I voiced my opinion of registering the business to incorporate it as a business, setting up the business bank account, and then finishing up with the other administrative details.

We all know how egotistical and stubborn chefs can be, especially when they are your partner (and also because he is my father). He wanted to start the business without a plan. In my mind, I wanted to use the months before the legal documents were prepared by Jane's legal team and the landlord to officially create a tenancy agreement to create a brand new image for the restaurant. Why did Chef Simon want to start the cafe immediately? He said it was an "auspiciously good date" for him to do so. In hindsight, he was right. Business is all about speed.

Short of a few hours from returning my staff pass and saying goodbye to all my colleagues before I abruptly started my entrepreneurship journey, I was caught up in a whirlwind of chaos. The entire restaurant was a mess. Jane had a lot of stuff in the restaurant to bring to her other outlets. It was a sight I could never forget: "Is this how my journey in business is supposed to be?" My morale was at an all-time low, and now I finally know why many say that entrepreneurship is not for everyone. Not many can stomach a chaotic start to their own business.

Jane got a lawyer to create a legal document to transfer the operations from their business to ours. I sensed relief when she finally rinsed her hands from this bistro; was there something she knew about Chef Simon that I did not? There was no talk and no plan to hire anyone when taking over a business with such short notice. Who else than your own family to recruit in such conditions? My mother joined the restaurant to help out Chef Simon.

My mother wasn't pleased - she was already enjoying her life, going for exercise sessions and hiking every day. One can say she has retired from the F&B industry; it was finally time for her to enjoy the fruits of her labor. However, with my involvement in the restaurant, she agreed to help. Her wish of taking over the restaurant one day came true, but the conditions were horrendous - sometimes, you can't have the best of both worlds.

The first day of operation started with an empty restaurant with no one allowed to dine in. Several customers who frequent the social enterprise came and ordered their food for takeaway. Jane was there on our first day to greet her loyal supporters. She was telling them that the restaurant was going to be taken over by Chef Simon and me and hoped that they would carry on giving their support to us. It was a professional gesture from her, and I appreciated it. The little things people do often have the longest-lasting impression on us.

All it took was a week of operating the restaurant, which gave me more insights into the F&B industry in the new normal. The days of dining in and having a good meal are over. Due to the paranoia of Covid-19, people have adapted to ordering takeaway in person or by a food delivery app. Like a software program, all it takes is a new version of the code and the behavioral patterns of human changes.

The first month ended, and balancing the books for the first month was a depressing affair. The numbers showed that we were losing money. With all the Covid-19 measures in place, there was an uphill battle to make it profitable. My mindset going into this was to make the business successful as there's a saying: "The best entrepreneur makes money despite the market conditions."

The Public Health Bureaucracies flip flop

Things started to look better during the next month. Public health bureaucracies eased up, and dining in was finally allowed again, with a maximum of five people per group. However, they added a brand new restriction to it: Covid-19 vaccinations.

Singaporeans who did not take the Covid-19 vaccination were not allowed to dine in; only ordering food for takeaway was allowed. A year ago, it was a restriction on my life with the mandatory face masks and social distancing. Fast forward one year later, and it is affecting my livelihood, my business, and the way it was operating.

With a brand new university term about to begin, Chef Simon and I were looking forward to having a boost in customers from old and new students alike. As expected, the first week when the university reopened was the best business week by far. Students and lecturers were flooding into our restaurant to order food; it was the kind of busyness that many F&B businesses expect. The restaurant was profitable in two months, an accomplishment worthy of praise. Within the week when the university reopened, my business began seeing good days after a terrible start.

As expected, the Public Health Taskforce announced that the cases were going up again, which made them rethink their existing measures; they wanted to tighten the health measures to fight Covid-19.

Less than a few weeks after allowing dining in for parties of five vaccinated people, they were going to limit the dining to parties of two vaccinated people. With social distancing implemented, one's business operates at half capacity while paying the same rent and utilities. With the number of vaccinated people per party limited, some establishments had only a quarter of their premises to accommodate their customers, or else they risk getting tormented by our friendly social distancing ambassadors.

It is pointless to blame anyone for the Public Health Taskforce and the public health bureaucracies mandated by them. Knowing full well that I agreed to operate a restaurant in the kind of market conditions the country was in made me accept the consequences of my action. The only way forward was to adapt to the measures to keep the operating overhead as lean as possible. Hiring additional staff was not an option, and upgrading my kitchen equipment was too.

There was a creeping sensation with the public health bureaucracies, and how the Covid-19 task force operated made me unable to sleep at night.

Imagine an environment where the free markets cannot operate freely. Instead, the government grows steadily and becomes so huge it can control every facet of your life. It can mandate mask-wearing the moment you step out of your home. It can authorize the usage of a mobile app to track every step of your movement by checking into an area. And it also has sovereignty over your own body; not taking the Covid-19 vaccination exiles the individual from participating in society. This centralized medical control wasn't happening in Singapore alone, with many countries doing that to their population.

Singapore's success as a nation led many to leave their home countries to seek prosperity and opportunities here. With the Covid-19 measures in place, these expatriates started to run in droves, citing that Singapore was no longer the place they knew.

In the shoes of an F&B business owner, the public health bureaucracy "easing and un-easing" was not helping the businesses. In the name of preventing the spread of Covid-19, public health bureaucracies exist at the expense of the real economy. Despite some sectors of the economy getting wiped out, other industries were thriving - the tech industry was booming due to the rising fad of WFH and the so-called "future of work." The healthcare industry with the Covid-19 vaccine demand led me to understand more about the wealth transfer mechanism where money flows from one place to another based on the market direction.

To add gasoline to the fire, the university changed physical lessons to e-learning. The students were to attend classes remotely, and most of the staff returned to WFH. In other words, what seemed to be a boom for my business became a nightmare with the university's mandate.

The Bootstrapped Cafe

Imagine this - a brand new cafe pops up in your vicinity, and walking past it weeks before its opening, you notice it is undergoing renovation. The previous tenant has closed its shutters, and a new aspiring cafe owner has stepped up to the challenge with the mantra: "My cafe is different from every other one!" Everyone loves cafe hopping; it has become Singapore's national pastime to spend time buying food or scrolling endlessly on their smartphones. A first-world country's measure of success is the amount of time wasted outside of their corporate jobs on useless activities that don't involve enriching their soul. A utopia envisioned by H.G. Wells.

What they don't tell you is the untold cost of this renovation. There's a reason everyone rational investor has always made their fortune from real estate, either from owning various real estate or creating an interior design consultancy firm. Every food business requires a location to begin; it doesn't matter if it's a brand new home-based business ready to sell you a new variation of diabetes or a food manufacturing company creating your favorite mass-produced sausages.

A typical food business generally scouts the market on a location depending on the type of product they are selling. In the case of a cafe, it is optimal to open it in an area where foot traffic is high. A location with high foot traffic is a recipe for a successful launch but not a long-term sustainable business. The number of new cafes launched means that in a year, a brand new one pops up next to you, selling the same avocado toast and latte as yours. Each time a new cafe pops up, it takes over the previous tenant's role and features the same product. The only exception is the renovation, giving it a brand new identity. Who am I kidding; it's just another form of "minimalistic" design, as the food blogs today have run out of words to describe the cafes. I know they are trying to paint them uniquely, but when every new food business popping up is a cafe, there's a limit to the description that a writer can spin up - despite being paid to write a feature article for them.

The renovation and the rental quoted to them make up the bulk of their initial capital for starting a food business. With the predatory nature of landlords, combined with the neverending demand for real estate by aspiring cafe owners, rental prices in vital areas have gone through the roof. Upon finishing the one-year lease, the landlord will tell the cafe owner they will increase their rent due to "market demand." Already putting in their life savings committing to their renovation and the clientele built up over the past year - it is a tough choice for cafe owners to walk over and not sign a new lease. Finding a new location and then committing to a brand new renovation process is too hefty of a cost; imagine each time a landlord raises the rent on you, and you have to repeat this step every time.

In the past year, there has been an influx of articles in the mainstream media talking about the rent of various places doubling - primarily in coffee shops where many hawkers have built their livelihoods. This act has led to many hawker stall owners not renewing their leases and going for early retirement instead. As a result, one key reason you see many new food businesses in Singapore popping up and then closing is due to the price of rent. One tenant may attain an excellent rental to entice them to take up the unit. However, nearing the end of the lease, the rental price goes up. The food and its price sold by the food business have already factored in the rent, utilities, cost of ingredients, and labor costs. Raising the rent will require the tenant to increase prices or reduce the portion. The former may lead to a significant drop in customers as the price of food is very competitive and a touchy topic for the consumer; the consumer can quickly go to another place offering the same food at a lower price point. The latter will lead to a slow decline in business over the new months as the customer base will notice the stagflation in real-time regarding the price they pay for the food, leading them to the same conclusion of going elsewhere to eat.

No matter how you think about it, it is a lose-lose situation. Most food businesses refuse to raise prices or reduce portion size. The business owner will pick the ultimate sacrifice, a lower profit margin, by paying more for the overhead. Many scenarios can run through their heads. The option of not carrying on the new lease with the higher rent requires them to move elsewhere to build up a new loyal customer base. Another option is to bite the bullet and carry on the lease to potentially gain more customers and improve the business due to their consistency.

Moving to a new location requires a coat of paint to renovate the cafe to look identical to its brand. There is also no guarantee that their "loyal" customers will patronize their new location. Of course, when you have public health bureaucracies being enforced and eased with a snap of the finger, running a food business when it already has a high margin of failure becomes an ordeal. Many business owners look at the micro situation of their business - price goes up because of rent or the ingredients due to the supply chain issue; they accept it at face value because the mainstream media reports it as such. There is more to it than raising the price because of these issues; the macro picture tells you everything you need to know. We will get into this in detail later on.

With this knowledge attained from experience, the way my restaurant functioned was as lean as possible. Taking a page out of "The Lean Startup" by Eric Ries, what the restaurant was before was the same restaurant it was after the handover. The cost of renovating for a short-term lease of fewer than two years doesn't justify the need to renovate it. I still have Chef Simon and his fantastic food as my product.

Most aspiring food business owners would stop me here and say: "You just don't want to spend money on renovation. You are just justifying your decision because of your short lease." Sure, go ahead with your renovation, and then when your landlord decides to double your rent, you will thank me for reading this book (if you did) and save yourself the headache of starting a food business. The current climate of things heading around the world, especially in Singapore, is pointing to every sign that the era of free-market capitalism is long dead. Small businesses will eventually go extinct as they are no longer needed to build up this country, and every corporation will become the private arm of the state. If you need an example, look at Grab.

My restaurant didn't even have a cash register. There is only a book to record the sales, handwritten receipts, and a QR code for customers to make payments. One good story that I remember from starting this business was the day a session was scheduled with the bank to have their card terminal installed. The social enterprise initially used it and recommended it to us. They used a card terminal issued by the bank and a payment system device by an IT company.

I scheduled sessions with both parties to find out more about them. The card terminal was a typical card reader which accepted debit and credit card payments. However, the cost of it blew my mind. There was a flat fee to be paid for the terminal, the best part of it all? It wasn't something one bought and owned; it was a lease to rent for a fixed term of a year before renewing the contract. If you thought this was bad, a 3% fee per transaction exists. Imagine this, you pay for a terminal to use it, and then the company issuing the product tells you in fine print that they will take a 3% fixed royalty from each transaction. Does this sound like a good deal? So the next time you visit a food business, and they don't have a card terminal to accept your payment, remember this.

The other product was a payment system - a typical SaaS (software as a service) product that tracks sales records. It doesn't function as a payment gateway and requires a separate terminal (from the bank) to transact card payments. Without sparing a second thought, the decision was an easy no.

Being extremely frugal with the initial startup capital to start a food business, coupled with the practicality of knowing the state of the market as it is enabled my restaurant to go through turbulent times. Like they say, prepare for the worst and hope for the best.

First Trip abroad in the new normal

Eight months passed, and the restaurant was able to break even every month. Most contrarians told me that food businesses can't break even until years into the business. It was finally time for me to go on my long-delayed business trip. My business partners agreed to meet in Turkey due to the lack of public health bureaucracies enforced. Coincidentally, Turkey has a name associated with it, the "Cradle of Civilization."

Since it was the "new normal," everything we knew about the world flipped on its head. Traveling used to be as easy as passing through immigration had many new health protocols. There were now pre-flight prerequisites to take care of before being able to pass through immigration. A pre-departure test before taking the flight was required. Booking the ticket was as simple as before, but the tests were troublesome. First, you book a session with a licensed medical institution before attending the appointment. Next, the test involves poking into your nose with a stick; I still remember the first time I took it back in 2020, and it made me tear up a bit. The final part is the results time; all it takes is for the result to make or break your day. If you get tested positive for Covid-19, the flight ticket bought for the trip would require a date change.

Imagine getting tested positive for some reason, the entire trip has to postpone, and you have to reschedule your flight and accommodation. We all know how inefficient some airlines are when one wants to reschedule a flight. In some cases, when booking a ticket close to the departure date, there's a policy that doesn't make it refundable or able to reschedule. Upon receiving the negative test, I sighed with relief. I could only imagine if the test came out positive for some reason and my entire trip would have to postpone, potentially wasting both my time and the people I was going to meet.

It got me thinking about something Chef Simon told me after the 9-11 incident. It seems more measures that complicate the human experience gets enforced with each new black swan event. One can only wonder what's next - Carbon Taxes to check if you have consumed more carbon than usual in the past month?

Arriving at Changi Airport to travel for the first time in two years felt surreal. I've always made weekend trips to Changi Airport with my family to visit Jewel Changi Airport, the flagship of Singapore's aviation excellence. I made my way to the check-in counter to get my luggage checked and to receive my flight ticket. The queue at the check-in counter was non-existent - nobody was traveling apart from the occasional foreigner transiting via Singapore. I saw less than ten local Singaporeans at the departure area, and the check-in process included a pre-departure test memo and the Covid-19 vaccination record as expected.

Going through customs was still the same as before and what awaited me upon entering the departure gates was an empty and silent retail area. After two long years of minimal travel and Singapore finally kickstarting its travel engines, the shops were closed - possibly waiting for the travel boom to get back up as an indication to resume business. The only stores opened were the convenience stores: 7-11, duty-free shops selling perfumes, liquors, beers, and makeup, and the food court. I went to the second floor to visit the restaurants I patronized on previous trips to see if the business still operated. Every single restaurant was closed, and even the sports bar was closed - that is a bad sign. Walking around the food area and noticing their posters offering promotions from a long time ago and not removing them told me that it has been a long time since these restaurants were open.

It was a different experience from two years ago when I traveled and saw every shop open and travelers actively going up and down the gates. The restaurants were always full, and I had a decent meal at a Taiwanese restaurant before the flight. Patrons at the sports bar would be conversing with the bartender and watching soccer matches together - ordering beer from the tap non-stop. Savvy travelers like myself would scoop up deals at the premium clothes outlets such as Tommy Hilfiger, where out-of-season shirts would be selling at a higher discount rate. Everyone has their views on wearing a mask. Most people wear it, and some don't. With our liberties eroded, governments worldwide have mandated it. Businesses seeing the green light from it have also started following suit by ensuring their employees wear one in the office. If wearing a mask enforced by your employer doesn't scare you, imagine what else they can do to you. This policy started to trickle down to various industries, and the airline industry became the first that wanted to be revitalized as soon as possible - doing whatever it took to get their planes off the grounds quickly. Embracing the measures practiced by the Covid-19 taskforce and enforcing them on their customers - the greenlight was passed by health authorities, and the airline industry was back in action.

The airline I was flying for enforced a mask mandate, meaning that every passenger on board had to wear a mask throughout the flight. A flight from Singapore to Turkey was about eleven hours, and the ordeal was not pleasant. Humans being habitual adapters, was quick to adapt to this mandate. On the flight to Turkey, after struggling to catch enough sleep as possible, I noticed that several passengers were not wearing a mask. My eyes saw that they were carrying a cup of drink, and that act was enough to make the flight attendants not bother them with putting on one. I followed suit and got myself a bottle of sparkling water, and the flight attendants didn't bother me ever again. So all it takes to beat a mandate is to carry some form of food, and the flight experience was back to what it was before the public health bureaucracies.

Istanbul Airport (IST) to the city center was not a long journey - it was about an hour by car. It was eye-opening to touch down in IST and go through customs to notice that the airport staff, even the immigration and police officers not wearing a mask. They weren't screaming down the necks of the passengers and just going about their day. Quickly leaving my luggage and bags at the hotel, I explored the streets of Istanbul to familiarize myself with the city and to find some food. The first place I visited was Istiklal Street, a famous tourist location with more shops per square meter. Police were on patrol on the streets, and some were on guard duty. Regardless, it was a breath of fresh air to experience the tail end of winter blowing in my face. The majority of people in the streets were not wearing a mask as Turkey has removed the mask mandate in public places, and seeing this made me wonder when Singapore will remove it as well.

I arrived a week early to explore the city and drink in the sights and sounds of a country I'd never visited before in my life. Eating Baklava, a Turkish sweet made up of a pastry filled with sweetened pistachios daily, led to my first toothache. Istanbul is a city that doesn't shy about having too little food to fulfill your gastronomic adventure. Taking the time to explore the city on foot was a great decision; Istanbul is a city where having a car would render one stuck in traffic for a very long time during peak hours. Visiting the old town of Sultanahmet to see the Hague Sophia and the Blue Mosque for the first time left me in awe - marveling at the architecture and the grandiosity of both places of worship.

Before making my trip to Turkey, the Singaporean news headline was talking nonstop about the inflation crisis in Turkey. If a small country like Singapore has its headline about Turkey, then you better pay attention; it is not every day that Singapore mentions Turkey. Not wanting to go into detail, the standard of living in Turkey has gone through the roof due to fiscal policies, and it was ugly.

Here's a story of my firsthand experience of the inflation crisis in Turkey. On my first day arriving in Istanbul, I went to one of these minimarts to get myself a bottle of sparkling water. It cost me roughly 50 cents in Singapore dollars. Three days later, I returned to the same minimart to shop for some fruits. To my shock, the price of the sparking water went up to 70 cents, a 40% increase in a few days.

I knew inflation was always a monetary phenomenon, but to have the price of an item go up that much was crazy. Before this incident, inflation in Singapore didn't rear its ugly head that much; objects don't go up in price that quickly and often. To have prices rise that quickly, and often in a country one calls home, is not the kind of country that would make one feel secure financially. Imagine the hard-earned savings and work that one has to endure to accumulate that kind of wealth, then to have a fiscal or central bank policy implemented to devalue everything you own. I could sense the panic in the streets as the locals looked visibly distraught. Being a foreigner, I felt stares at my back, and I knew I had to be on my guard.

Russia-Ukraine Conflict

Another big global issue in the form of the Russia-Ukraine conflict was brewing in the distance. My family was checking up and sending messages throughout my trip telling me to stay safe; a combination of an inflation crisis and a potential war was not a good feeling when one was far from home. Being close to the conflict meant that I had to immediately go back home to Singapore as soon as my meetings concluded. With my plans to visit other cities in Turkey scrapped, my return flight was pushed forward to the next available date.

Arriving at IST in the afternoon for my return flight, a bustling airport with travelers greeted me. Unlike Singapore, where entering the airport was seamlessly smooth, there was a check from entering IST through a short pre-screening. Another round of pre-departure tests awaited me due to Singapore's strict re-entry requirements for its citizens, and I had my nose brutally abused by the PCR test. Going through the same emotional roller coaster of waiting for the test result made me feel uneasy- if I tested positive would render me stuck in a foreign land, and being unsure of their health protocols wasn't good. After a couple of hours, the test came out negative, and I was all cleared to take the flight back home.

IST has one of the shiniest and most glamorous decors when it comes to airports, but unfortunately, the food offered wasn't the best. Defaulting to an international brand was the safest play. After spotting Shake Shack at the corner, it wasn't a tough decision to have it. After having my meal, I went to the boarding gate to head home.

There was a relief when the plane touched down back in Singapore when the pilot announced: "Welcome back home to our passengers from Singapore." I quickly grabbed my bag and left the plane. My family was extremely pleased to see me back home and prepared a hot bowl of noodle soup. Did I mention how hard it was to find Chinese food in Istanbul? It was a bittersweet welcome back home to strict public health bureaucracies. I had to self-quarantine at home for seven days, with an exit-swabbing test awaiting me before I could return to society.

Spending seven days at home wasn't that hard, being the type of person who can sit idle and work on my computer or read books. There was plenty of time to plan for the next year or two, the time I didn't have when managing my business. The trip to Istanbul made me realize how fortunate I am to live in Singapore.

There were two sides of the same coin: Turkey, where public health bureaucracies were non-existent, and Singapore, where the protocols ran rampant. Why did Covid-19 restrictions "not work" in Istanbul? Was it because the Turkish people were uncontrollable, a population of free-spirited humans, who couldn't give a damn about what the Turkish government was to impose on them? After spending a week in Istanbul, I could finally see why some countries were having protests and not caring about the Covid-19 restrictions. With their nation's monetary crisis in chaos, the wages earned by their people were essentially worthless, with the prices of food going up nearly every week. The Turkish people had no reason to care about Covid-19 when their financial situation as a country that affects their livelihoods is more catastrophic than the virus itself to care! Istanbul, their primary business center, was already having such an issue; one can imagine how bad it can be in other rural states in Turkey.

Alfred Henry Lewis stated in 1906, "There are only nine meals between mankind and anarchy." The current situation of the country doesn't look good.

How about Singapore? With the country being a financial powerhouse, as a nation, we are prosperous. Our population cares more about keeping up with the Joneses than anything else. With an abundance of food options, clean streets, and a properly functioning government at our backs, the only we worry about is how to virtue signal and look good on social media. A friend once told me that a sign of a prosperous country is one with fountains and lights shined on it.

With no monetary crisis as disastrous that mirrors Turkey, Singaporeans have no problems in their lives. So what do you do to manufacture something to change their thoughts? Impose public health bureaucracies and give them meaning to their lives. With the old Singapore eroded and systemically replaced with sky-high towers of public housing projects that Singaporeans don't own, a future dystopian smart city is well on its way. There are two sides to the Singaporean dream, one where you subscribe to the kool-aid of it or one where you wake up from it, realizing it's a nightmare. Just as I thought the crisis affecting Turkey was only a phenomenon in that country, it started growing like a plague far more deadly than Covid-19 across the world, and the worst has yet to come.

The next phase

Reality seems to be a Hollywood movie. From daily reporting of Covid-19 infections and death statistics being blasted everywhere on mainstream media platforms and the occasional "expert" from institutions giving their insights on the issue, there is always a massive fear campaign on-air for the whole world to see.

Humans, having adapted through the ages, started seeing through the official narrative and questioned whether this Covid-19 thing was a decoy for something bigger. I remembered the day public health bureaucracies started becoming mandated. Within the next week, the drink stall at my staff canteen started the "cashless movement" - citing that cash could carry the virus on it, WOW! They then implemented cashless payment options with the SGQR (Singapore Quick Response Code), making every transaction digital. Many were happy with the "adaption" by the staff canteen. I, being the contrarian, knew there was more to it than meets the eye. I often made small talk with the stall assistants in the staff canteen, and from what I can gather, they didn't implement the cashless option because they wanted to; it was mandatory for the organization itself.

It's funny how things all start to seem coordinated when you can see the big picture - removing the cash option was to ensure the mass adoption and digital enslavement of the world by slowly conditioning them. Covid-19 stuck on the cash notes was the pretense given to entice the world not to use it. Months later, new "experts" appeared on mainstream media outlets to talk about how they were wrong about cash being able to transmit Covid-19. It was too late, as the masses conditioned themselves to use their PayNow and PayLah apps on their phones. The day Russia invaded Ukraine was when the script changed. Covid-19 was no longer the sexy girl in the red dress the media was selling. They were pushing Vladimir Putin as the villain of the world. The President of Russia is now the new bad guy, the central figure, the one we all hate. Shortages and food crises started in Sri Lanka, and the rest of the world followed suit, with some countries exporting less of their commodities.

And exactly like how the Covid-19 campaign started, the mainstream media relentlessly published stories and deployed their anchors to talk about how Vladimir Putin was responsible for all the shortages in the world! What the? It was as plain as day that it was a manufactured lie, but the response from it shocked me more than what the news was saying. The general population, the people I interacted with, and the consensus became anti-Russian. From being worried about Covid-19, everyone around me started to forget about the public health bureaucracies, which changed our livelihoods, destroyed businesses, and caused the wealth to shift from our hands to the ones who planned it and stole the life of our youth.

The Public Health Taskforce started to remove most of the Covid-19 restrictions. The heroes of our times, the Stool Pigeons and the Warden Pigeons, were all being fired from their cushy jobs. Contact tracing and wearing of masks in public were gone. Everyone was happy with the effective management and decision made by them. The mask era is over. Singapore is back to the days it once was before March 2020, or is it? Shy of the two-year mark when the nation collaboratively put on a mask in the name of fighting Covid-19 together, it marked the end of this social experiment. Although everyone celebrated the "freedom" returned to us, the question mark remained unanswered: "Is it not us that decides what we choose to do?"

The day the public health bureaucracies eased up was one to remember. A regular customer visited my restaurant with a few of his friends. It was uncommon for him to eat in a group, and as they walked into the shop, they were happy they got their freedoms back. It was a cause of celebration, the look on their faces filled with glee.

It was a pleasant occasion to catch up with friends after a long time. On the other hand, it was depressing to see people celebrating the "freedom" bestowed upon them. This "freedom" is a birthright given to us from the day we were born. The fact people celebrated it made me realize that we are no longer "free" as a human. There is a saying that humans live with amnesia, and they can't remember what we had before Covid-19 became our reality. And after living through the Covid-19 era, simply moving back to what once has become a privilege.

It is also a worrying trend that the return to normalcy and thinking that Covid-19 restrictions were "behind us" shows the population's dependency on an entity apart from themselves. This lack of ownership over their lives is going to be a problem moving forward.

Like the passing winds of change, Singapore has achieved another momentous victory. Another one added to their history books of success.

The craziest inflation

The humans with amnesia roaming the streets moved on with their lives. Worldwide it was also the same thing. Slowly every country removed its public health bureaucracies, and flights abroad resumed. No one seemed to care about Covid-19 anymore and had forgotten what happened during that era.

With the restrictions gone, the central planners have accomplished their goals - the era of digitalization of everything and lockdown conditioning. All of a sudden, as the world moved past the Covid-19 era. We entered a brand new one where the demand for everything surged back to what it originally was. That spelled bad news to everyone. Amongst your friends, there is a common consensus - the prices of groceries have gone up. Eggs that used to cost less than two dollars for a tray at the supermarket have gone through the roof, costing three dollars a tray. On a micro level, things were getting more expensive; the uncle next door was crying desperately: "Things are going more expensive. Why is this happening?"

The humans with amnesia on the streets have forgotten about the lockdowns all over the world. What does a lockdown experience a typical Singaporean experience? We have the cushy WFH and remote work offered by their organization; going to the office usually results in a letter written by the employee to report them to the Ministry of Manpower for not respecting the chance of spreading Covid-19. Here's the best part, lockdowns in Singapore don't matter that much. The lockdown experience in Singapore is like night and day compared to other countries where they produce the real stuff that the world needs, like energy.

Glorified paper pushers in our financial services economy, with their remote work and WFH policies, can afford to sit at home and pretend to work by watching Netflix. The real economy is energy. The ones in the oil and gas industry, the coal, steel, coffee, and orange juice you drink, and the food you eat, to name a few. In other parts of the world, lockdowns also exist. And the result of that is far worst than one can imagine. Sure, you lock down a bunch of paper pushers in first-world countries like Singapore, and it doesn't matter. But when you enforce lockdowns in countries where they produce energy, that is another story. That is catastrophic.

With the lockdowns in place, the amount of workers working is incredibly tight. I remember the clean streets during the first wave of lockdowns in Singapore, the air was fresher, and the roads were cleaner - what a time to be alive. Looking back now, it was a complete disaster from an economic standpoint. With the streets and roads empty, what does that mean? The demand for energy goes down, and so do the commodities. That leads to companies producing having the demand for their products lowered. Their workers are no longer required to work. Coupled with the insane money printing and stimulus money sent out in the US, workers who got displaced are receiving "free" money. Imagine a society where you get money even when you don't produce, in this sense, a version of Universal Basic Income (UBI) in its Beta version.

Singapore isn't a country not known for being rich in natural resources; we have to go to the extent of importing our drinking water from Malaysia. That means when prices of oil & gas go up, we can only sit and watch as the prices balloon. Higher oil and gas leads to more expensive production of commodities such affects the entire supply chain. The world suddenly went into an inflation overdrive, with the US having double-digit price increases for most of its products. Pumping gas at the petrol station was no longer cheap, with the price of oil going to the moon.

Even though the inflation crisis started appearing worldwide, it didn't matter until Malaysia announced a ban on exporting fresh chickens to Singapore. As usual, the mainstream media created a fear campaign by interviewing stall owners selling chicken to give their views on this issue. Singapore's national dish was the Hainanese Chicken Rice, and cooking it with fresh chicken was part of the secret to the dish's taste. With the ban on fresh chicken from Malaysia, using frozen chicken or an alternative source for these hawkers was required. Not every hawker was open to the idea of using frozen chicken, citing that the taste would become horrible. Some hawkers even thought about taking a break and closing their shops until the chicken ban ends. Some other hawkers started dabbling into new ideas and pivoting to selling other food. The chicken ban was a success. With that announcement, every Singaporean visited a nearby chicken rice hawker shop to have a plate of chicken rice (possibly for the last time?) before the ban started.

Inflation wasn't done with our nation yet - businesses have been trying to avoid raising prices. For the past few months, food businesses have been looking for alternative suppliers offering the best price for their goods. The global supply chain was in shambles, with the lack of crops and fresh foods produced and harvested - a direct cause and effect of the public health bureaucracies. No matter how hard these food businesses attempted to avoid the inflation issue, it was finally time to do it. A food business cannot survive without making tough decisions.

The first few food businesses that reacted fast to raising prices were the hawkers selling chicken rice. Rental is at an all-time high, and they cannot afford to close their shop. Chicken rice hawkers started looking for fresh chicken from Australia and using Kampung Chicken to carry on operating their stalls; no surprise that these suppliers were charging incredibly high prices for their chickens. The suppliers were not dealing with one chicken rice hawker; there were more than a hundred of them who wanted them too. With the supply fixed and the demand going up, the chicken prices skyrocketed upwards,

My experience regarding inflation post-Covid-19 in Singapore manifested in my business operations. For my business, the COGS (cost of goods sold) started rising during the first few months of 2022. The price of salmon went by nearly 20%, a sizable percentage increase. Not looking at a percentage increase is a big mistake most people make. Imagine chicken rice priced at $3.50, and with the chicken ban coupled with the need to source new chicken sources at a higher price, the chicken rice has a new price tag of $4.00. Some might say: "Hey, that is only a $0.50 raise, no biggie!" If one puts on their thinking hat and looks at things from a percentage point of view, that is not just a 0.50 cent raise - it is close to a 15% increase in price!

Consequences of rising prices

Chef Simon was not the most talkative man in the room. Like most men from his generation, he would often try to remain silent unless needed for him to give his comment. The memories of Chef Simon conversing with chefs from other countries has opened my eyes to how a professional conducts himself. I remember when I was younger, and often when talking to my friends, I used to interrupt them in the middle of their speech. Everyone knows from experience that interrupting someone is a rude thing to do. Years of watching Chef Simon's conduct and demeanor taught me a lesson or two to become a better listener than a talker.

Having my phone ringing throughout the trip to Istanbul from Chef Simon caught me off guard, as he wasn't known as a person who spends all of his time texting. Knowing that something was amiss, there was no way I could ignore his messages. He was noticeably upset and alarmed by all of our suppliers raising the prices of their supplies. This time around, particularly in March, things started to go sour. The prices of some of our items went up, not just by 1-2%; understandable and justified because the Monetary Authority of Singapore, Singapore's central bank, reported the annual inflation rate was around 3%.

This time around, prices went up from a minimum of 10%! Some supplies were going up by nearly 20% to even 30%. Chef Simon questioned the suppliers on why the prices were going up astronomically high. As usual, with the standard canned answer directed by their bosses, the sales representatives cited the Russia-Ukraine issue as the reason behind the surging prices. When every supplier gives the same response to the reason behind the crazy price hikes, you know something is amiss. Unfortunately, the entire Singaporean population believes in the official narrative of Russia being the Eren Yeager of the current conflict. Having massive campaigns and corporations siding with Ukraine in this conflict, it was as though Covid-19 became replaced with a brand new rallying cry - a brand new mission for Singapore to rally behind as a cause to unite the nation as one.

Running a business has its woes - such as managing your labor cost, reducing the existing overhead to make it more profitable, and creating new products to attract new customers. However, outside of the business's control is the rising cost of the overhead, in this case, the rising prices of supplies.

The plan was supposed to absorb the rising prices. Despite our suppliers raising prices at the start of 2022, Chef Simon and I decided not to increase ours. In March, upon returning to Singapore and having an emergency meeting with my team - we decided to raise the prices of our products. We could no longer look away from the insane price hikes. The choice to secure a business's profits is way more important than anything. My experience a year ago from meeting the retired finance elder made me acknowledge the importance of my decision.

The moment we raised prices at the end of March 2022, we could see the turnover rate dropping. Some customers noticed the price hike and carried on patronizing us. Some were visibly upset with the rising price, making it the last time they visited. Many business owners would question their decision, and the "paper hands" would revert their actions to make their customers return once more. I stood steadfast by the decision made; even though we were the first to raise prices in this crazy world, I knew it was the right move. We were early to make this line of play; our neighbors would eventually have to raise theirs.

The 4D chess move I made paid dividends. In June, when the Malaysian ban on exporting fresh chicken began, the prices charged by chicken suppliers went through the roof. Singapore's food industry relies on chicken, with the general population enjoying eating Chicken Chop, Chicken cutlets, to name a few. As a result, the demand for frozen chicken went to the moon; every food business had to compete for whatever chicken was remaining in the pool. Every food business, from hawkers to cafes and restaurants, had to raise prices a few hours after the chicken ban went live.

Years of playing card games at the highest level and thinking of the most optimal play made my business move a success. It was finally here, the craziest inflation of my lifetime, with some analysts saying it might be the worst one of our lifetimes.

I am no financial expert, but running a business and seeing inflation affect my business, combined with having the time to educate myself on what's coming next, has made me perceive the writing on the wall for the food industry and the world as a whole. With corporations controlling our private affairs and the state controlling the public side of our lives, we are slowly inching close to the end game where we will own nothing and be happy. Just like the WEF (World Economic Forum) announced.

In a properly functioning economy, lockdowns and unproductive jobs wouldn't exist. Just look at the job scope of these Stool Pigeons and the Warden Pigeons and their salaries; the people I met in Turkey would want to swap positions with them. Easy money with no effort required? A perfect recipe for a job for a lazy person. Don't get me wrong, these people working these useless jobs didn't start as lazy;

they are your typical next-door neighbor whom you greet every morning.

Initially motivated and inspired to rally the nation to fight against Covid-19 by taking up the job of a Stool Pigeon/Warden Pigeon, they slowly became corrupted by the authority given by the role. What happens when you give a random person power? A simple look at history would show you how power can corrupt anyone. With their newfound power, these people could brandish them to instill fear and compliance in anyone with whom they deemed not contributing to the good fight of curbing the spread of Covid-19.

While they are not contributing to the real economy, their job essentially destroys what remains of businesses and the markets. This fact is also not limited to the Stool Pigeons, but the Warden Pigeons paid to sit and watch people check in via their contact tracing application. Another form of the Covid-19 gig economy is the swab tester, and as you guessed, gets paid to do a mindless job by jabbing people's nostrils with the test kit to see if they tested positive or negative for Covid-19.

The short-term damage of the wealth transfer from productive labor to unproductive labor is a call for concern, but the long-term damage to the population's psyche. People don't realize this is one big social experiment where the masses undergo conditioning to work meaningless jobs.

A career used to mean a thing for some. But with Covid-19's appearance, many people's careers were affected, resulting in them taking up these gig jobs. These gig jobs have replaced the human desire to forge forward for a life worth living. Instead, they now live in fear and beg the central planners to help them.

Retirement in Singapore

A brand new form of a gig job came into the picture - private security guards. A job that many elderly folks were taking up. Imagine this, the elderly taking up these jobs. In our minds, security jobs are roles taken up by physically active and fit people. How are the elderly supposed to protect us physically? They can't possibly run as fast or fight as rough as they compared to when they were younger.

The truth is; these elderly are taking up these jobs because retirement has become impossible. From birth to the last day of their careers, the Merdeka generation of Singapore has contributed their lives to working a job. Many have achieved success in their careers and attained a degree of financial health, allowing them to retire in peace. However, not everyone from the Merdeka generation achieved this ideal lifestyle. Our founding fathers knowing the importance of savings created the Central Provident Fund. The CPF system is a compulsory savings account that every Singaporean must contribute to from their income.

The CPF has a growth rate of 3-5.5% annually, depending on the individual's age. After hitting a certain age, these individuals can draw money from their CPF accounts to fund their retirement. This system sounds good on paper, but unfortunately, not everyone's retirement lifestyle is the same, some might not want to travel all the time, and some might want to enjoy a quiet one. Financial savvy Singaporeans know that the CPF is only sufficient to sustain the bare minimum lifestyle you would have upon retirement. If one desires a better retirement, such as a skiing resort trip to Switzerland annually, one needs to build financial assets to sustain that lifestyle.

Unfortunately, most of the Merdeka generation lacked financial education unless they worked or educated themselves in finance. Who can blame them - they have spent their lives building up this country. The fear kicked in when their lifestyle during their careers, such as maintaining that luxury car and annual trips to Europe, were no longer possible upon retirement upon checking their CPF accounts. Not to criticize the Merdeka generations for being unable to retire, but I believe the future generations of Singaporeans will also face this reality. Why are Singaporeans unable to enjoy retirement? Just look at the astronomically high prices of everything going up. The answer given by everyone will be: "Inflation." But what is inflation?

What is inflation?

Inflation is the expansion of the money supply. And how is the money supply being expanded? My generation of Singaporeans believes in stability and security. This "stability" and "security" is a mindset instilled by their parents, who never had to enjoy Singapore at its peak since they were the ones building it from the ground up. A long time ago, some guy selling toast and coffee as a hawker could raise a family of ten children. Fast forward to today, the same guy in the role cannot do so. Ten children? They can't even raise two kids, let alone themselves!

As the public sector in developing countries starts growing, more money is being taken from the hands of private individuals to maintain their country through higher taxation. And in some cases, the printing press (central banks) will expand the money supply to keep it going. First, it starts slowly by justifying the need for more regulation to protect the consumer. Next, it grows faster and faster by creating new governmental agencies and hiring more civil servants, resulting in an artificial demand for these unproductive jobs. When productive labor gets directed towards a sector that doesn't produce, such as the public sector, the cost of everything will increase. Rising demand without the hands on deck to meet the supply of goods & services always cause sky-high inflation.

With the security and stability sought after by my generation, nothing screams these values other than taking up jobs in the public sector.

Talk to an average Singaporean regarding their career prospects, and the response would be to aspire to work in the civil service. What they don't realize is that their mindset of joining the civil service means that their need to fuel government will increase, potentially resulting in higher taxes from its citizens or more money printing from central banks to fuel this machine. The next generation would have to pay it forward with the decisions made by the previous one, a never-ending cycle of misery.

The private sector functions in this way: demand and supply. A fixed supply can't meet higher demand for it, and the only way to increase supply is to higher more hands on deck to fuel it. More supply means that the job created is economically sound and leads to higher revenue for the private enterprise. Higher revenue means the ability to create more jobs, and more jobs equal more goods & services. The demand and supply ratio is maintained, and all is well.

In the civil service, one has to understand something. The public sector doesn't create anything. It distorts the demand and supply ratio by creating agencies to create new regulations for private enterprises, and these regulations will affect the cost of running a business. The cost of producing Product X may cost Y dollars, but with the new mandates created, Product X now costs Z dollars. Coupled with the increased demand by a non-productive labor force created in the form of new civil servants, Product X costs ZZ dollars.

I don't believe the Singaporean government is the perpetrator of all the fiscal turmoil Singapore faces today. That's a shallow way of putting things in perspective. Singapore became a success in fifty short years because of its policies allowing the private sector to grow while having a just government with sound economic policies. The hard work of the pioneer generations of Singaporeans paved the way for this nation because they took up the "hard jobs" in the private sector. A good example is the construction and commodities sector. I believe the pioneer Singaporean government knew what they were doing, and there is only so much they can contribute as their successors might have a different goal from theirs.

The problem lies with the stability and security that the average Singaporean seeks. Ask an average Singaporean whether they want to work in the private sector, and they will answer you with a resounding "NO." They then blame foreigners from abroad for "stealing" their jobs. How are these foreigners allowed to "steal" these jobs when Singaporeans don't want them in the first place? These jobs are the ones the Singaporeans willingly give away because they refuse to work a job with overtime. These foreigners would take up roles not wanted by the Singaporeans for lower pay and reap the benefits of living in Singapore. The new foreigners are living the Singaporean dream, and they would then bring their families here, seeking a new life for themselves. I understand the mentality of these foreigners as I've seen what life is like outside of Singapore.

With the snowball of "safety and security" pursued by the next generation possibly going through the roof by the end of the decade, this means increased inflation for all, and nobody will be able to retire. So what is the end game for this nightmare scenario? No one is to blame - the Singaporean government can't do anything but increase the number of jobs in the public sector to meet the demand of their safety-seeking population, or else they face trouble in the next general election. With more public sector intervention, the private sector has to absorb more and more new regulations created by the "woke" Gen Zs' who has forgotten the principles that our founding leader Lee Kuan Yew wanted us to inherit.

Understand Cycles in Society, what is the End Game?

Singapore has only known a life with a strong and prosperous government. One investor, Jim Rogers, who coincidentally lives in Singapore, has a book I read often. The book's title is "Adventure Capitalist." He mentions a quote by Plato in the book regarding democracy and how it always goes through a cycle. This cycle starts from an oligarchy to democracy to chaos, and the cycle repeats itself. Coincidentally, he used this quote when he visited Singapore at the turn of the millennium.

He cited Singapore as one of the biggest successes of the past century due to the rule of Singapore's "absolute and authoritarian" Prime Minister Lee Kuan Yew. Singaporeans live in an era of hard work and foundations built by the pioneer Singaporeans and the founding governments. Unfortunately, this generation and future generations of Singaporeans are taking things for granted. With no understanding of the path taken by our founding fathers and the lack of tough times to endure to look forward to a brighter tomorrow, our prosperity will eventually come to an end. As they say, there is no light without darkness.

Plato's quote hits harder when one is a student of history. Past European empires often had a strong emperor or king who built the empire from scratch. Initially starting as an empire that benefited its citizens, it eventually falls sideways slowly but surely as the founder passes away. As time passed - policies and taxation increased, the masses' dependency on the state, and the ages of chaos restarted.

The USA is the empire that emerged at the end of the two world wars, with the whole world respecting them due to their military might and their currency as the world's reserve currency. That day will come when their time at the top ends, with speculators and analysts starting to see the writing on the wall for them. Which country will come out on top when the dust settles and becomes the world superpower at the end of this decade?

The bigger question one needs to ask is: "Does it affect me who becomes the world superpower?" I have found that ignoring the biases and news pushed by the mainstream media has made me a much happier and more focused individual.

In the past, when we didn't have smartphones, our lives were much more peaceful and blissful. The only people we knew were our neighbors and our family. That allowed us to live more meaningful lives and benefited our immediate communities. As a result, every community started to flourish, and people trusted each other organically.

With communities displaced and replaced by online interest groups and the rise of the virtual world, we are becoming connected and "online." Not having the ability to be alone means that one does not have the time to be in solitude to keep one sane. Even with more technology and "improvements to our livelihoods" combined with the mantra of ending poverty and creating more opportunities for everyone on this planet, why are our quality of life decreasing and the cost of living going up?

What is the end game with sky-high inflation? What will the world look like in the future? Let's take a trip to a world where equality exists through the technological endgame.

Let's take this journey together, shall we?

CHAPTER 6: THE WORLD IN THE NOT-SO-DISTANT FUTURE

DISCLAIMER: This section is a work of fiction. Unless otherwise indicated, all the names, characters, businesses, places, events, and incidents in this book are either the product of the author's imagination or used in a fictitious manner. Any resemblance to actual persons, living or dead, or actual events is purely coincidental.

"IT IS 8 AM. PLEASE WAKE UP NOW!"

"IT IS 8 AM. PLEASE WAKE UP NOW!"

The smart clock rang its alarm, signaling the start of the day. Charles woke up from his bed groggy, possibly from the effects of having too much alcohol last night. Fear grasped his chest as he recalled consuming too much alcohol would harm his smart score. Charles's heart stopped as he looked toward the top corner of his vision.

The top corner of his vision showed a clean green "70/100" on it. Feeling relief, he stepped out of his pod and walked toward the bathroom. A green score meant that Charles was still in the green. Lion's Hub is the city he chose to live in after Singapore implemented the new smart city plan to divide the country into various hubs of both smart cities and towns. Waking up early today, Charles had a free morning to himself. Later in the afternoon, he had to take a flight to Europe for a meeting for a brand-new demo of his organization's product.

"Charles, would you like the same type of shower?" A voice blared out, engulfing Charles. It was a voice that only he could hear.

"Yes, please proceed."

The voice went away, and the shower head started its rhythmic shower for Charles. The aromatic smell, combined with the water therapy, was a perfect start for Charles's day. All seemed fine until the water stopped, and the same voice spoke.

"Hello Charles, the water supply has been temporarily stopped. Your beloved neighbors have overused the utilities this morning. If you wish to continue your shower, please pay it forward with your carbon credits."

Cursing his breath, Charles stepped out of the shower. "If it is for the environment, then forget it." Carbon Credits, the new system where one can purchase them to indulge themselves in activities that can potentially "harm" the environment, were a novelty for average citizens in Lion's Hub. Costing up to a whopping 100000 XGD Credits, it was close to a year of annual wages for an average citizen. Given that the governor of Lion's Hub has pledged to uphold the "zero carbon footprint" that his predecessors before them have, the entire city operated without emitting too much carbon to save the planet from a total collapse. All in the name of an environmentally sustainable future. Charles wondered how the previous generations could live their lives being complete savages; they were responsible for the reality he was living in with the high skyscrapers and technologically augmented reality. How could his ancestors live such indulgent and climate-destructive lives, to the likes of cultivating their crops, having their own families, and driving their gas-guzzling vehicles? Having their crops and rearing their animals meant that the carbon output of these activities was actively contributing to the collapse of the world!

Remembering the day cows were outright banned a few years ago marked the new world order. It was the end of eating red meat(curse that unholy meat) and the taxation of cows being alive (how were cows taxed as they can't use a payment processing system to pay their carbon taxes?)! Those unholy and indulgent activities of the past reinforced the iron mind Charles had to live a life of meaning; to ensure that history wouldn't repeat itself. How could people even stomach the taste of meat; it was as good as eating the flesh of another human being!

The meeting that Charles was to attend later in Europe was a product demonstration of a brand new type of food to be included in the upcoming Lion's Hub's "Sustain 4Ever festival". Sustain 4ever festival is the annual emerging technology and sustainability conference held in the heart of Lion's Hub, Zero Carbon Hall, for companies to showcase their new products for the citizens to see. The organization that Charles worked for was named Meatless to Meat, and its goal was to transform recycled materials into the "meat" of old, to create a new use case for recycled materials. Charles was particularly interested in the plastic chicken patty; he had never consumed plastic before led to his interest. The food consumed in Lion's Hub was grown and made in labs. All in the name of upholding the pledge of zero carbon emissions. The mere fact that humans did not try to consume recycled materials in the past was mind blogging; how could they not try to innovate and think of new solutions for things? Instead of partaking in innovation, these savages were destroying the environment by carrying on with their "traditional" habits.

Looking at the clock on the wall, he still had time before heading to Europe for the meeting. Feeling a bit hungry, Charles decided to have a meal at the nearby Lion's Canteen to have his favorite meal - The Roach Burger.

The Lion's Canteen was the brainchild of Roachie Wong, the most famous sustainapreneur of the last decade. Roachie was born from nothing and rose to the top after a short stint working in a company specializing in meatless technology from the old world. Roachie Wong joined several international clubs to pitch his ideas for a post-meat world. Not wanting to repeat the mistakes made by the savages from the old world, Roachie created a startup, Lion's Diet, to forge a brand new future where the food consumed by humans wouldn't harm the environment.

Being instilled by a vision of consuming bugs, Roachie designed the Roach Burger, made of cockroaches and genetically modified to taste like burgers from an international franchise, Mcdonald's. Being the ever-eccentric sustainapreneur, Roachie was infamous for his diet of consuming meat. He swore he needed to shoulder the burden of consuming the diet of the old world to remember the past. Lion's Canteen is a retail food shop that expanded from Lion's Diet, primarily used as a biotechnology incubator for creating new food products from alternative sources.

Lion's Canteen

With the bright lights and chatter amongst the patrons in Lion's Canteen, Charles found himself a lone table to occupy. Within a split second of him sitting down, a humanoid zoomed into his table at lightspeed. Charles looked up at the humanoid and instantly recognized the humanoid - it was Roachie Bot 3.3!

"Good Day, Citizen Charles. One order of The Roach Burger will be served to you immediately.", Roachie Bot 3.3 spoke out loud after scanning Charles's personal AI before zooming back as quickly as it arrived at his table.

Ordering food in Lion's Hub has made life easier and seamlessly less taxing on the individual. Roachie Bot 3.3 is a brand new invention by Roachie Wong after several iterations of creative destruction to create the ultimate humanoid companion powered by AI. With the vision of "Selling Roachie Burger a thousand times in a minute." Roachie designed the Roachie Bot to do just that. Being a student of history, Roachie studied the long-lost traditions of "Cha chaan tengs" in Hong Kong, a type of food institution akin to fast food - without the aircon. Roachie understood having a patron look through the menu and ordering it from another human in the form of the service staff was something he could disrupt with his disruptive and hacking abilities. He decided to remove the entire human interaction of ordering the food via the service staff and replace it with a technology that was only available with the innovations of his fellow disruptors, a humanoid powered with AI.

Roachie didn't aim low - his vision of a thousand burgers a minute wasn't simply just something he said - it was a conviction to reduce the amount of carbon footprint by human conversations that could potentially save the world from a climate disaster. It took him 32 trials and iterations to finally get the humanoid to work, ending the trials at the 33rd version; he decided to call it the Humanoid 3.3. The idea of integrating the personal AI of every citizen to connect to the Humanoid 3.3 was the missing key to making the vision of Roachie's into a reality. On the night of running through the slides and presentation to present at the Sustain 4Ever festival that year, he had an epiphany. His long-dead idols like Resla Nicole, Alberta Finstein, and Stephanie Jobs were people of the past; Roachie wanted his legacy as a legendary inventor to remain immortalized, hence he decided to name Humanoid 3.3 after himself, Roachie Bot 3.3. His innovation became a city-wide phenomenon upon release. Every citizen in Lion's Hub was amazed at the innovation and thought process behind the Roachie Bot 3.3. Knowing that the Roachie Bot 3.3 can minimize the number of human interactions via carbon footprint was the one thing that pushed its massive adoption.

Charles could remember the design philosophy of Roachie Bot 3.3 and their illustrious founder and inventor, Roachie Wong. Having watched and become a cult follower of Roachie Wong since he was a young citizen, he could remember every product launch and speech that Roachie gave at every Sustain 4Ever festival. The popularity of Roachie Bot 3.3 resulted in a 3.3% decrease in carbon output from the annual Lion's Hub Carbon Report! In the name of saving the world, it reduced the number of interactions among citizens to a bare minimum. Charles understood the importance of the impending climate disaster. Hence, the reason he made it a commitment to donate some of his XSGD Credits to Lion's Diet so that Roachie could use them to develop more climate-saving products.

Staring at the final bite of The Roach Burger was a sad feeling in Charles's tummy. The Roach Burger was the most delicious meal since the Plant-based Chicken Rice he had at the nearby Sustain-ocourt. Only at Lion's Canteen could Charles have cockroaches cooked to perfection, with the Roach soup not tasting up to par with the Roach Burger.

"Maybe I should order another Roach Burger since they don't serve this in Europe." Charles contemplated. Instead, he walked around the city before taking his rocket trip to Europe.

Walking in the city was a favorite pastime of Charles's. He saw various shops selling products from lab-grown paper-printed chicken wings to recycled rubber beef balls. However, a word of caution would come if Charles were to partake in too much shopping - it was a habit he was trying to fix as it had dire consequences if he pushed it too far. He recalled with dread stepping into the Gaia Facility due to his past actions. Since then, Charles has sworn to uphold his pledge. The mere thought of it sent shivers down his spine.

The Gaia Facility

The Gaia Facility stood tall in Lion's Hub as a reminder for its citizens to remember the privilege of living in paradise instead of those ruins outside of it. Failure to uphold the rules and pledges would result in attending a session based on the severity of their actions. Gaia Facility looms in the background of Lion's Hub. A symbol of reverence is associated with these giant buildings. Its size as the largest tower in a city; makes each citizen tense up looking at it from a distance. Growing up in Lion's Hub, Charles often heard stories from his fellow citizens about the things that go on there. Every citizen that relocates into Lion's Hub has a smart contract to authorize: with rules and regulations in the terms & conditions to agree to before being christened as a citizen - one must undertake on oath and be implanted a microchip in their right hand.

With the microchip implanted, the citizen has assimilated into the smart grid. One must uphold their conduct as a proud citizen of this technological marvel. Some laws of the old world inherited by the country he is in, Singapore, have strict measures regarding chewing gums. With chewing gum banned in Singapore, it naturally passed down as a mandatory rule in Lion's Hub.

The other laws in the smart-contract put in place by the almighty governing body are as follows.

"Number 1: To respect everyone regardless of their pronouns" - every citizen may be biologically of one gender, but as humanity has progressed, the "old sciences" are no longer relevant. Males can be called females. Females can be called males. Sometimes they have no gender and can label themselves as it/they/them or some cases, be a human with the pronouns of a cockroach.

"Number 2: Sustainability above all" - every citizen must pursue a project or initiative to push the drive for a cleaner, greener city. Proceeds and profits from their work must go to the governing body in the name of anti-capitalism. Profits are the bane of humanity and the source of all greed.

"Number 3: Medical assessments to keep everyone healthy" - every citizen must undergo a bi-weekly medical checkup with their body technician to submit their daily health readings from the sensors in the microchip that can detect irregularities. A monthly vaccination schedule is given to each citizen so that the health standards of each citizen are secured. Failure to comply with the vaccination schedule will result in the citizen being expelled from Lion's Hub and forced to relocate back to the old world.

"Number 4: No time for solitude" - Lion's Hub's integral motto is for everyone to be equal and happy forever. The governing body created the Lion's Pack, a social welfare community agency that creates daily events. Participation in these events is compulsory for citizens during their free time to keep them enriched and occupied. In the name of productivity - no time can be wasted on an idle thought, for the brain must be active at all times.

"Number 5: Consume in the name of the future" - Learning from the old world and their self-indulgent catastrophic behaviors will lead to the eventual demise of the earth. Citizens of Lion's Hub are not allowed to consume anything that comes from animals. Production and farming are no longer needed anymore. Materials become recycled as food sources in the name of a sustainable future.

"Number 6: To uphold the peace" - Citizens are all responsible for their actions, being the moral compass and role models for the savages of the old world to emulate and look up to as inspiration to give up their decadent lifestyles. A citizen is encouraged to report a dissident citizen to their nearby Gaia Facility for re-education if they deem them "socially destructive." Nothing stands in the way of a citizen of Lion's Hub to maintain peace, prosperity, and progress for their city.

It's been several months since Charles underwent the re-education program at Gaia Facility. Hence why he could remember the rules so vividly. The Gaia Facility was a work of art and progress even though it was supposed to be menacing and fearful initially, and it wasn't as bad as he thought it would be.

The big question was how Charles even got admitted into it in the first place. There was an incident where Charles finished his meeting early and had some time available. He headed over to Lion's Canteen to enjoy a Roach Burger. After having one Roach Burger, Charles was still hungry and ordered another. At that moment, his personal AI started to emit a burning sensation - warning him that one more act of self-indulgence would lead to his admission into the Gaia Facility. Knowing the consequences, Charles ordered another Roach Burger and consumed it with carnivorous might, an act seen as defiance against the technocratic gods of Lion's Hub. A behavior worthy of being called - a savage from the old world. Within seconds, a siren played overhead - citizens in the Lion's Canteen shuddered in fear. Dread and fear filled the eyes of those citizens who understood it, while curiosity filled those who were oblivious to it. Sirens, a mechanism used to signify an event out of the norm, is a relic not used in the days of Lion's Hub due to the eternal peace achieved from ridding themselves of the habits of the old.

"BANG! BANG! BANG!"

There was a sound of knocking outside of Lion's Canteen. Within seconds, the citizens all started to act like children. Was war imminent? Was a famine coming?

"Impossible, the innovation and sustainable goals have rid the world of all the strife and demons which used to haunt our ignorant ancestors!" that was the worst thought that filled the minds of the citizens upon hearing the knocking. Everyone froze up, unsure of what to do next. When suddenly Roachie Bot 3.3 started to turn back on, the voice of serenity changed to a sinister one upon the boot-up sequence, and that's when the Service Manager of Lion's Canteen bit his lips.

"They are here."

"EXECUTING ORDER 13! EXECUTING ORDER 13! CITIZEN SHOWING SIGNS OF SAVAGERY!" the eyes of Roachie Bot 3.3 turned golden, and the voice became one of reverence, filled with authoritative might. Instantaneously, Roachie Bot 3.3 zoomed twice as fast as it would move to take an order from a patron towards Charles!

"What the…!"

Before Charles could complete his sentence, several Roachie Bot 3.3 surrounded him and unleashed an electronic sensor pinning him down to the ground with his hands automatically tied behind his back! Charles then realized that the Roachie Bots' sent a signal to the microchip in his hand to override his bodily functions. There was no fighting chance. Being microchipped and linked to the grid meant the citizen could not escape!

The Shepherd arrives

"…Well, well, well. What do we have here today." a tall and suave-looking man walked toward Charles and looked at him confidently. Even the Roachie Bots were standing with their heads bowed at the presence of this man.

"Ah, it seems you have willingly acted out of the rules of being a citizen of Lion's Hub, citizen Charles." The man was reading a report generated in thin air, aerial 3D printing - a marvel of Lion's Hub's innovative prowess.

"Excuse me? I just had an additional burger. What's wrong with that? Not like I committed an act of treason!" Charles was visibly angry and told the man off.

There were gasps of shock from the other citizens watching the exchange between Charles and the man. The citizens knew who the man was, and how did Charles not know? What a savage he was! This man standing before Charles was none other than Mars Tan, a Sustainability Correction Officer, a true hero of justice. The latter stood for sustainability, a net-zero environment, and an actual role model for the citizens of Lion's Hub. As a graduate of the National University of Singapore's Climate Citizen Ph.D. program, a program famously known for having a 0.69% admission rate, enrolling and graduating from this program would almost guarantee a role in the governing body of Lion's Hub. Direct admission to be a central planner and ruler of Lion's Hub attracted the very best that Singapore has to offer.

Mars appears in Holo-TV, the television broadcast network in Lion's Hub. As well as being a frequent guest on radio shows that each citizen listens to, with the microchip playing it. He knew that Charles was due for re-education. As a practitioner trained in the arts of NLP (neuro-linguistic programming) and wanting to be a benevolent role model to every citizen in his presence, he knew he had to pick his words wisely. Mars used his Lion Interpreter Enhancement, a state-of-the-art AI only accessible to Sustainability Corrector Officers, to enable Mars to run through various scenarios in the cloud to find the best possible answer to any dire situation.

It has been ages since Lion's Hub has had any form of deviant behavior from its citizens as there was no need for rebellious or individualistic behavioral tendencies anymore since the city fulfills the needs and wants of everyone.

Eureka!" Mars had run through every possible scenario and was ready to handle Charles properly.

"Citizen Charles, I understand your predicament. His Excellency Roachie Wong has done an amazing duty for us by creating the Roach Burger. Your actions of consuming more than the daily quota per person mean that someone in this city would not be able to have one."

Mars spoke with understanding, applying the advice from his Lion Interpreter Enhancement to behave like a politician from the old world.

"To meet the sustainable present and future for each citizen of Lion's Hub, it would be wise for you to act accordingly. The future citizens are looking at us as their role models." Mars knew he had it in the bag, but he still had one more coup de grace up his sleeves.

"Ah, I understand now. Dude, you are making me feel shameful for my actions." Charles stood back up to leave Lion's Canteen.

"Citizen Charles, thank you for your cooperation. Shall I take you for a cup of Soy Latte nearby for your time?" Mars knew that it was the ace in the hole.

"Sounds great. Let's do it."

Knowing that the alternative was to attend a community event, having a Soy Latte with Mars was the better deal, and little did Charles know that it was the worst possible decision.

"What a complete fool!" Mars thought to himself as he ushered Charles out of Lion's Canteen. Looking at his armed guards next to his Resla Model: Lion, he gave them a nod, and the guards knew where the destination was going - Gaia Facility.

Resla Model: Lion, a state-of-the-art electronic vehicle created by X Ash A Twelve Musk, the current Chief Sustainability Officer of Resla. The young Musk has inherited the will to lead Resla into the future. Its siblings are also part of Mlon Eusk's kingdom of technology - the siblings being more preoccupied with the development of SpaceZ to colonize Mars to ensure Earth's resources do not get depleted by us pesky humans. The Lion model was a commemorative design created just for the governing body of Lion's Hub to use, using only the finest raw materials from the old world, crafted to represent the prestige of owning a gas-guzzling vehicle. One might ask, gas-guzzling vehicles? Isn't using oil & gas the bane of the entire sustainability movement? It is, hence with the benevolent might of Resla and the governing body of Lion's Hub, that the ones leading the world are to carry on the traditions of the old world. Not wanting to share the electronic charging stations and needing to be anywhere on demand as the main reasons, the vehicles used by the governing body were all using the technology of the old world - those environmentally destructive gas guzzlers. However, the citizens were aware of the sacrifices of the Resla Model: Lion. A necessary evil to remind them of the acts made by the savages of the old world.

With the windows programmed to block out the view outside, Charles had no idea where he was going. However, he knew that Soy Lattes' are incredibly hard to find (and cost a lot too for the average citizen). The only beverage he consumed regularly was NEW water, a type of water produced using recycled materials. The other beverage Coca-Cola is the only surviving drink with a history.

"We have arrived." Mars could no longer hold on to the chuckle and gave out a bit of laughter. Charles didn't sense anything wrong with Mar's demeanor and was honored to have sat inside the Resla Model: Lion. It was a rare chance for a citizen to ride in one without being part of the governing body.

"What in the… What's going on?"

Charles felt his vision losing focus as he left the car. His consciousness faded as the microchip in his hand received the mandatory signal from the walls of Gaia Facility - to prepare him for judgment.

Was it a few minutes, perhaps hours, maybe even days? Charles wondered as he woke up lying flat on an operating table. His first reaction was to sit up, but his body couldn't move - the microchip in his arm had overridden his body's natural movements. A feeling of dread overcame his body, but his body couldn't move.

"Where was I? What happened to the Soy Latte? Where is Mars?"

Charles was astounded by the reality right before his eyes. From a distance, he heard footsteps approaching. It was Mars, and his face contorted with terrorizing glee.

"Looks like you have awakened. Welcome to Gaia Facility, you filthy citizen on the brink of becoming a savage!" Mars unveiled his true persona. His voice changed into one that of Adolf Hitler, drunk on power.

"No. No. NO! You made a mistake. Get me out of here! NOW!" Upon hearing Gaia Facility, Charles panicked, his face turning blue, with tears starting to well up in his eyes.

"Citizen Charles, you have willingly agreed to join me in having a cup of Soy Latte. Remember that you have already received a warning before controlling your insatiable hunger in the name of Lion's Hub. Do you not remember the pledge? Having a cup of Soy Latte meant consuming three straight meals without delay. That makes you savage now!" Mars' little trick of baiting Charles worked.

"YOU! I can't believe you tricked me!" Charles was angry and scared at the same time. Nobody ever lived to tell the tale of admission into the Gaia Facility.

"Now, now. Let us begin with the rehabilitative procedures to ensure you learn a lesson from this."

"Wait… NO!!"

The Gaia Facility went into overdrive, and the AI in Charles's hand in the form of the microchip started to perform a sequence causing Charles to go through an insurmountable amount of pain. The pain made Charles not remember any of the punishment he received.

After what seemed like forever, Charles remembered waking up in the middle of the night in his bed. He tried to recall the events before blacking out. To no avail, he could not recall what happened - only one thing stuck to his mind, the image of Gaia Facility.

Just the thought of that massive facility made him shiver.

Traveling redefined

The travel hub was a short distance from Lion's Canteen. Traveling in Lion's Hub is a breeze with the amount of self-driving EVs available. The trials and tribulations of going through the crash and the amount of venture capital poured into the funding of self-driving cars was necessary advancement for the human race. History lessons of Lion's Hub emphasized educating young citizens on the chaotic destruction that took place ages ago before the creation of smart cities. With self-driving cars being a reality, flying cars shortly became mainstream, and the ease of traveling became democratized.

It was a far cry from the days when owning a gas-guzzling vehicle was accessible to the rich & famous. EVs, as the vehicle of the new world order, have become adopted rapidly. Corporations and public housing projects have EV charging stations everywhere. The days of gas stations were far behind us all. With massive budgets being planned and allocated towards a sustainable future, humanity has found the cure for gas guzzlers - one step closer to achieving a net-zero carbon present. Past monopolies have all gone bankrupt. They either merged or rebranded themselves. These monopolies faded in time, and the citizens of Lion's Hub have quickly forgotten about the climate-destructive actions of their history.

Taking an EV was simple - a split second of connecting the brain to the cloud was executed by closing the eyes and linking the microchip to Harry-AI. Harry-AI derived its name after the founding father of Singapore. Harry is the unofficial English name of Lee Kuan Yew and was strategically used by GovTech to immortalize the legacy of the eternal ruling family, the Lees. Since each citizen had a microchip implanted, they were all linked to Harry-AI, the ever-encompassing stature of dominance. After connecting, the mere thought of hailing an EV would summon an available EV nearby toward the citizen. The EV would no longer need more commands; it would easily download the location where the citizen desires to go from Harry-AI. Humans are no longer required to think and make decisions, as Harry-AI is watching and knows your every move.

The Travel Hub was a massive transport terminal filled with

different EVs - from vehicles for short distant commutes in Lion's Hub; to bicycles and even the Resla Rockets. One might wonder, what is a Resla Rocket? The Resla Rocket is the reason behind the death of the aviation industry. SpaceZ is a company associated with Resla, a pet project of the eternal innovator, Mlon Eusk. After performing several launches with SpaceZ to colonize Mars with his rockets, he came to a Eureka moment when his rocket could be better suited for international travel instead.

After several iterations and countless sacrifices (both literally and figuratively), the Resla Rocket was ready for business. The initial reaction to the Resla Rocket wasn't great - the savages of the old world did not embrace the idea of sitting in rockets that took off at warp speed. Who knows? Maybe they would become jelly due to the crazy take-off sequences. Due to massive outrage and public response to the Resla Rocket, it became a failure. Mlon Eusk was not discouraged, calling the savages nothing more than sheep, the same kind of sheep that fell for the Dog-coin and Bitcoin scam years ago. With the introduction of smart cities, the Resla Rocket became a reality. A pivotal point in history divided the savages and the citizens, the former choosing to carry on living their decadent lives of being gas-guzzlers.

The Birth of the Climate Warriors

The citizens being almost cult-like members of the Resla and SpaceZ hype train, worshiped the grounds that the Musk family stepped on. The first inhabitants (first citizens) of city projects had the same ideology - believing in social welfare to create a sustainable future for all. They became the first governing body after being selected by their respective countries governments.

Swearing their loyalty towards Mlon Eusk, stemming from their days in the old study known as liberal arts, the first law signed into the cities was to provide funding towards the mass adoption of the Resla Rockets and every EV in existence. One might ask, who provides the funding? This funding came from the citizens who chose to live in the cities. Instead of taxation (an ugly word used in the old world to treat the savages like serfs), the brand new term invented by the governing body was called "climate crowdfunding."

Climate crowdfunding became enacted into the smart contract by every city. It is a compulsory fund that every future citizen must contribute from their income. The savages of the old world were vehemently against the "Climate crowdfunding" scheme that the first citizens were planning. Due to the control of the media, these voices drowned, and the citizens all agreed to it. The road toward Resla adoption was not easy. Resla could not reach its goal of climate crowdfunding to manufacture its EVs. Citing the "Climate crowdfunding" evasion tactics used by the citizens, the executives of Resla ordered the governing bodies to create a digital currency. A digital currency that worked only from within the smart cities to ensure that each citizen contributes to their fair share of the "Climate crowdfund"!

The governing body launched a smart-coin system using the existing blockchain technology. This smart-coin system was similar to the CBDC (central bank digital currency). Cash lost its use, and banks had to close.

A brand new governing agency emerged, the Sustainability Monetary Fund. The agency's sole purpose was to handle every affair related to the smart-coin system. Taking a page out of the central bank's playbook, it hired 69 new PHDs annually to give it a status of importance and reverence. With the introduction of the smart-coin system, the EV push began. The endgame of sustainability has arrived. With the smart-coin system, each citizen has to. It was a win for the smart cities' sustainability goals and an even bigger win for the Musk family.

With the never-ending funding by the citizens and the belief in a better tomorrow through EVs', Mlon Eusk doubled down on innovation. EVs went from zero to a hundred in a few short years, and the demand went through the roof. Smart cities started to become colonized - the same way Mlon wanted Mars to be.

The Supreme Being

One of the biggest hurdles was to remove the need for the steering wheel. Citing "true innovation is where the need for driving one no longer exists." Resla started doubling down on its testing to create a future where self-driving cars would become like its namesake: self-driving. Mlon's vision of self-driving was to become as seamless as sitting inside the vehicle, taking you to where your heart desires.

Early models of Resla cars all had steering wheels; the primitive Resla models had little autonomous driving abilities and could only automatically steer for a few seconds. Mlon knew he had more work to be done. The conditioning from limited auto-steering was insufficient in social engineering. After countless deaths, sacrifices, and funding in the name of removing the steering wheel, years passed, and the flagship model of Resla was ready. Appropriately named the Resla Model: Smart, it had everything a climate warrior could only dream about: made with strictly recyclable materials, no longer using those climate-destructive lithium batteries, and 3D printed with absolute precision. The smart cities rolled out the Resla Model: Smart as the true autonomous EV. Savages of the old world who were once part of the "self-driving race" could only look on and marvel at the sights and grandiosity that Resla achieved. From self-driving cars, Mlon Eusk took Resla from a meme stock to a company respected by his cult members and fellow climate warriors.

In typical fashion, Mlon Eusk has been officially christened "His Supreme Being" by the governing body. He was no longer supposed to be called Mlon. The governing body mandated that Mlon and the rest of the Musk family be called "Supreme Beings." The early citizens saw it as a joke, considering April 1st (April's Fools Day) was the day it became mandated. Despite that, the governing body was serious about giving their god, Mlon Eusk, a title to thank him for innovation after innovation in making the world greener. On one fated day. As Mlon, I'm sorry, His Supreme Being was attending the award ceremony to accept his title, a lone man waltzed in through the crowd and unveiled a gun!

"BAM! BAM! BAM!"

Three loud shots erupted, and His Supreme Being fell to the floor. His Supreme Being, Mlon Eusk, seconds after being immortalized as the eternal god, was murdered in cold blood. The grid with all the smart cities in them went into full-on despair.

However, the governing body responded instantaneously to His Supreme Being's death (almost as fast as the coordinated response to Covid-19 by public health officials worldwide!), citing that the need for microchipping would need to be accelerated to connect everyone to the smart city. The research and unveiling of the modus operandi of the gunman revealed that he operated within the gray area. He hid from the cameras and was left undetected until he carried out his heinous attack.

With Resla achieving massive success by the "Climate crowdfunding" mandatory for all citizens, there was no longer any need for this climate crowdfunding program. However, the governing body was reluctant to give away its power to take a slice of the citizen's pie. As the saying goes, there is nothing more permanent than a temporary government measure.

Climate crowdfunding became the Climate Tax. One would have gasped at the idea of taxation, given that it was a scheme disliked by the savages of the old world. However, the citizens approved and praised the government for their brand new initiative; the thought of hating something savages disliked was akin to savagery - what they hated would be what the citizens would embrace. With "climate" in the name, what is there to dislike about Climate Tax?

The Climate Tax became official and signed into an accordion on April 1st (again). Each citizen was then mandated to contribute to the building of the microchip system. The design of the microchip system was to link each citizen to the city, their every thought, move, and action would be tracked and saved on the blockchain. With the release of the microchip, smart cities took another step forward with their plans of "saving the earth." Climate-destructive behaviors became a rare sight. EVs were programmed to only bring you to where you are allowed to go in a smart city. The technological utopia was complete, and one thing was left to control.

The food consumed.

The Travel Hub

"We only have The Supreme Being to thank for this life." Charles thought to himself as he checked into the travel hub, ready to catch a Resla Rocket to Europe.

Europe, once a continent of several countries, was significantly different today. Some countries have chosen not to be a part of Europe and have resumed their nation's identity. It was such a shame as being part of Europe has always been a beacon of progress, a shining unity of countries shedding their nationalistic roots for one in favor of a shared goal of saving the earth from a climate disaster.

Finding a suitable and comfortable seat next to the window, Charles settled into it. The chair was made from sustainable materials and was a state-of-the-art revolutionary innovation.

"We will be ready for takeoff in 15 minutes, kindly fasten your seatbelts."

Resla Rocket is the ultimate disruptor of the aviation industry. The aviation industry was once associated with airplanes and several airports. These airplanes were the devil's spawn, outputting more carbon than a climate warrior can even fathom. It called for a massive overhaul of the industry as the general population became more "woke." Trying to turn the airplane design into one not based on oil was not going to work - the testing, prototyping, and even the R&D were not cost-efficient solutions. As the woke population started to get more rowdy and angry at the airlines and plane manufacturers, politicians seized the chance to implement a Carbon Tax to tax the carbon produced by these airline companies! The Carbon Tax worked wonders. Demand for new airplanes dropped to the floor. Profits by the airline industry were at all-time lows as travel prices were far too high. The Carbon Taxes imposed meant that the cost of travel doubled, and the average joe could no longer take an hour's flight to Malaysia for under a hundred dollars; it was now close to five hundred dollars!

The woke mob still wasn't pleased; they wanted cheap travel with the carbon tax. Citing that these capitalistic monsters should reduce the profits and make it "cheap again," it was one of the pivotal overhauls in an era of "cancel culture" during the last days of the old world's emergence.

The Supreme Being, Mlon Eusk, sensed blood in the water. The Resla Rocket changed from its original design of going to Mars to becoming used for international travel. With some testing and changes to its design, the Resla Rocket became approved for use. The aviation industry became dominated by Mlon Eusk. Every airline manufacturer now worked for Mlon Eusk, becoming the Mlon monopoly. Mlon then set his sights on the various airports and worked with government officials to scrap their current usage of airplanes. With airplanes out of commission due to the insane demand for Resla Rockets, there was no longer any use for airplane runways. Using the Climate crowdfunding bestowed upon him by his worshippers in smart cities governing bodies, airports were all repurposed into travel hubs. Shopping and restaurants closed as nobody checked in hours in advance as the Resla Rockets only required checking in minutes before take off. Shopping became a pastime of the old world as citizens no longer partake in them - spending time in the metaverse was more conducive to them. The ultimate takeover of transport with EVs and the Resla Rocket was complete.

"We are ready for takeoff. Citizens on board, please take your Resla Pills to have the best experience for this trip. Thank you, and we will be arriving in Europe shortly." the voice overhead was played, signifying the start of the Resla Rocket.

Within seconds, the Resla Rocket blasted into the skies. Then it reached the clouds. And finally, into the stars, the moon, and the quasars. Charles is enjoying a psychedelic experience after digesting the Resla Pill. The sheer speed of blasting off, together with his mind going through the ecstasy of sensational pleasures, was a combination that made traveling from Lion's Hub to another smart city way more pleasurable than the days of taking a plane and suffering from turbulence.

"We will be arriving in Europe in 5 minutes."

After the voice recording ended, the passengers in the Resla

Rockets whipped out their smartphones to quickly snap pictures of them in space. Charles strategically picked the seat next to the window and viewed the entirety of space just by turning his head. Praising The Supreme Being by playing his hands together and making a prayer, Charles looked out into the great beyond, thanking the climate warriors for taking the steps towards a net-zero present.

The entire Resla Rocket trip from Lion's Hub to Europe took only thirty minutes. It took three minutes longer than usual due to a slight delay from a previous rocket scheduled beforehand. International travel has been cut short to less than a fraction of how long it took with the Resla Rocket. Going from one continent to another was a fast and quick experience that didn't require hours in advance. Using the microchip branded in the hands of the citizen, connecting to Harry-AI, and booking a Resla Rocket was as easy as imagining it in their heads. Payments processors are integrated seamlessly with the XSGD and Smart-coin system.

There was no need for customs or immigration officers with the travel hubs. Microchips in the arms of each citizen meant that traveling across various cities would be instantaneously recorded and scanned beforehand. The grid comprised various sensors interconnected everywhere.

Body temperature scanners in the microchip tracked every little action, such as going to the toilet and the amount of urine passed out. Each citizen can then check their hydration level based on the data collected.

Scanners also tracked reproductive activities. Citizens participating in the act could check their heart rates at the end of the session to see if their vitals are in the healthy range. In the era of smart cities, reproductive activities were no longer "reproductive." Babies were "birthed" from bright pods after manufacturing, the latest field of technology pursued by sustainapreneurs. Babies could be customized from a fetus and designed to look like anything their parents want; think of designer-made babies who could grow up to be the next Bollywood heartthrob.

This technological marvel also applies to international travel as well. Walking into the travel hub would instantly capture the face of the citizen. Making plans and validating the tickets were settled instantaneously just by walking into a travel hub. Before landing at the destination, the smart grid will update the citizen's ledger containing his travel log. The Harry AI of Lion's Hub would contact the master AI of that smart city and transfer the necessary information to the citizen to make his experience in the new smart city seamless.

Climate Lockdowns

It was an odd afternoon when Charles arrived in Europe. The city he came to was called Euro Hub. However, the streets were empty, with most of the shops closed. Charles checked his schedule, and it seemed that the meeting was still on. With a city this quiet, it seemed like a scene out of a zombie apocalypse. And then it suddenly clicked with Charles. Unmistakably, there was a reason Euro Hub was empty. It was an act made by the governing body of Euro Hub. No, not just of Euro Hub. Every governing body across the cities had created this new mandate, learning from the mistakes committed by those pesky savages of the old world.

There was an event a long time ago where a deadly virus appeared and caused the savages of the old world to go through a paradigm shift. However, the savages refused to learn from their mistakes. They didn't believe there was a deadly virus at all! The governments collaborated and tried different ways to mandate the movements of their population to curb the spread of the virus. However, the individualistic spirits of the human race refused to bow down to the liberty-destructive ways of their governments. What happened next was a massive awakening from the masses, as they realized that their governments were using the deadly virus to usurp more power from their people. Whatever happened to serving the people?

There were two camps to this deadly virus. The first camp was where people refused to give up their freedoms. And the other, the "useful" camp - how useful were they? They believed in anything the government said. Whether the government decreed an event regarding racial discrimination or a deadly virus, they would support that campaign. If a climate crisis became imminent, they would support it wholeheartedly. Any support from their end that could virtue signal their good intentions, these "useful" people would instantly rally behind it! It gave them great credence to support "the current thing." This group became the original climate warriors, the fervent supporters of The Supreme Being (Mlon Eusk) back when he was nothing more than a Dogecoin pumper.

The liberty group wanted nothing to do with the smart cities and the technological utopia the climate warriors envisioned. When the deadly virus concluded, both groups went about their ways. The climate warriors went about their desire to set up smart cities. The liberty group carried on living in their world outside of the designated areas to be redesigned into smart cities. The climate warriors reminisced about the old days of their beloved governments using the might given to them to induce lockdowns on the population. They loved the lockdowns and people not roaming the streets, producing more carbon that could harm the world!

Taking a page out of the government introducing lockdowns to curb the spread of the deadly virus, the climate warriors started the Climate Lockdowns initiative when they attained power. The Climate Lockdowns were the new iteration of the virus lockdowns started by their beloved governments. In the name of climate change, the climate lockdown was a monthly affair where cities in the grid would take turns shutting down their city to save the earth. It was a nationwide holiday, with every shop closed. Companies were not allowed to have their employees go to work. Consumption of food was not allowed during the lockdown.

You must be wondering - NO FOOD WAS ALLOWED? - how ridiculous is that statement, one must think? Every citizen was mandated to be fasting during the climate lockdown. There were no exceptions unless they were part of the governing body.

The governing body was allowed to participate in the climate lockdown; they worked overtime to ensure no citizen was caught not participating in the lockdown. During their overtime, the governing body indulges in mountains of meat and seafood. To them, a day of lockdown is a day of celebration. They follow a creed in inverse to commemorate climate change as the biggest fight of their lives.

Throughout the history of climate lockdowns, there were moments when the citizens would voice their opinions on how harsh the lockdowns were. Not being to eat and leave their residence goes against their human rights. Human rights were a belief that the savages of the old world hung on to in the name of protecting their liberty. The governing body sensing that this could lead to a meltdown of their control decided to take swift action. These citizens were rounded up and given an ultimatum. No one truly knew what happened on that day of that climate lockdown. Some theorized that these "brave" citizens were sent to Gaia Facility and never heard of again. Some even wondered if these citizens even existed. Nobody knew the truth. It became a taboo subject to speak against any mandate the governing bodies have put out and enforced - the coping mechanism in the citizens would reason within themselves: "The governing body will always do what's in the best interest of its citizen! Right?"

Charles got to experience the climate lockdown in a smart city as a spectator for once. Being the eternal planner, Charles would schedule a day of fun and games in his private metaverse server. That meant a few months of saving up his XSGD to buy a remote server. These remote servers cost a fortune for a mere citizen. Having an isolated shard of the remote server meant one could charge it and use it to their heart's content anytime. Even during climate lockdowns, when the grid went down. It was a surreal experience being out and about when another smart city had its climate lockdown. His XGD credits were still available, but the question was: "Where can Charles spend it as everything is closed?" With nothing available, every shop closed within the nearby proximity of Euro Hub's Travel Hub. Charles had nothing to do except wait for the scheduled Resla to take him to his meeting.

A few hours passed, and the meeting was finally over. "Ah, it's midnight now. Everything should be open now." Charles thought to himself as he exited the meeting, saying farewell to his colleagues from Euro Hub. It was finally time to explore Euro Hub at midnight, and he could find himself a place to destress, have a meal and explore the city in the wee morning. The lights started to pop back on. Like an electricity grid, Euro Hub brightened up like a light bulb. It was a beautiful sight to see. The buildings lit up floor by floor, ending with beautiful fireworks with sparks flying at the top. A blimp flew overhead above Euro Hub.

"THANK YOU FOR PARTICIPATING IN THIS MONTH'S CLIMATE LOCKDOWN! WE ALL HAVE A PART TO PLAY, AND YOU JUST DID!"

The blimp's overhead speaker played the recording, and the citizens in Euro Hub clapped their hands in excitement, almost mechanical-like.

Finding himself in a pub, the next scheduled Resla Rocket taking Charles back to Lion's Hub was at 5 am sharp. Jetlag was no longer an issue due to rapid advancements in the field of pharmaceuticals; anti-jet lag pills exist to acclimatize consumers to a different timezone. With the next Sustain 4ever festival coming up in a few weeks, Charles had to touch up and finalize the presentation to unveil their latest product.

"Meatless to Meat" is the company Charles worked for, and they are finally ready to unveil the product they worked on for the past years - the Plastic Meat Burger. Using only the finest recycled plastic for packaging, the Plastic Meat Burger intended to disrupt and out-innovate Roachie Wong, who was sure to appear at Sustain 4Ever festival to reveal his latest food offerings. Charles's CEO, Peter Lee, attended the same schools as Roachie, with both of them not liking each other and having a natural distaste for how they approached their revolutionary food ideas.

However, Charles had a master plan in sight. With the launch of The Plastic Meat Burger, Charles would be given the limelight during the product showcase. The truth was, Charles never liked Peter. He has always been a fanboy of Roachie since he first moved into Lion's Hub. Pledging to one-day work side by side with Roachie, everything he endured, suffered, and sacrificed (in the name of climate change), were all in the goal of standing, not next to, but with Roachie in the limelight. Charles's lifelong dream was within his grasp, and Meatless to Meat was just a mere stepping stone.

Sustain 4Ever Festival

The day has finally arrived. Lights and holographic imagery filled the skies. Charles has been waiting for this day since he graduated from university and vowed to take center stage as the new sustainapreneur of this generation. It meant the world to him to attend his first Sustain 4Ever festival. It was also a pivotal moment in his life to meet Roachie Wong in the flesh. Only ever attending the festival digitally with his Resla Goggles, the virtual experience is nothing compared to physically attending it.

The Sustain 4Ever festival will feature the most sustainable products ever created. Innovation comes second as the theme for citizens has always been saving the earth and fighting climate change. This festival will be a week-long event, with carnivals, music shows, and even a culinary competition as part of the festivities. The history of this festival stemmed from The Supreme Being's (Mlon Eusk) wish to create a holiday that would give the cities an identity synonymous with it.

Growing out of the mold of New Year's Day, Christmas Day, several Holidays celebrated by different religions, and even Labour Day, to name a few, announced that spirituality is dead. Smart cities built their foundation in the name of science, a complete 180 from the old world. Citing their accomplishments in the name of sustainability and innovation to improve the lives of their citizens, The Supreme Being cast away all notions of traditions and ushered in a new era where the human spirit became unhindered by the societal restrictions of religion, beliefs, and morals. Nothing was more important to the citizens of the cities than only believing in themselves as Gods - Gods of their technological reality. The governing body (who worships The Supreme Being like a cult member) introduced carnivals of games and all kinds of booths for the citizens to have fun. Music Shows where the very best music and entertainment idols from the virtual world would give performances. The one thing citizens enjoyed most was the culinary competition. It featured humanoid chefs whipping up food.

One might ask, who funds this Sustain 4Ever fest? Silly you, it is funded by none other than the climate tax! Who pays the climate tax?

The citizens! There's an adage - "People are only generous with their cause with money funded that is not theirs." So much for talking about the future of equality when the practices adopted are ones that plagued the previous generations.

"Greetings to all esteemed citizens. Welcome to Sustain 4Ever Festival!" Roachie Bots of several different models were zooming around in the conference hall.

Stepping inside the iconic Shangri-Eusk, the city's premium boutique hotel, Charles breathed in the sights and sounds of his first Sustain 4Ever Festival. It was a long time coming - from escaping the slums of the old world to pledging himself by branding the microchip in his arm to signify dedication to the cause of sustainability. It was a surreal experience attending the festival, and what was more astonishing to him was being inside Shangri-Eusk.

Shangri-Eusk is a collaboration between a long-time hotel conglomerate from the old world and The Supreme Being. In the business world, it is all about making friends and making money. There was no chance The Supreme Being could look away from potentially making a great deal with the titan of the hotel world, hence offering Shangri-La an olive branch to build the ultimate sustainable hotel in the smart cities.

To quell the potential backlash that The Supreme Being and the governing body (who signed the memorandum to allow construction of the hotel) from Shangri-La's involvement in smart cities, the hotel announced that it would be built solely by Resla and SpaceZ engineers. Citing the need for sustainable development using materials not harmful to the planet, it was an easy sell by the ones in power to convince the citizens of its development. Shangri-La carried on business as usual, using the same construction materials and their construction teams to build the hotels. And The Supreme Being was tasked with selling the dream by attending various shows to sell the concept of a sustainable hotel before his untimely death. And with that, the Shangri-La in the cities was all developed under the name of Shangri-Eusk.

Shangri-Eusk has been the home of Sustain 4Ever festivals since.

The hotels created by several home-sharing companies and technology companies seem like amateurs to the Shangri-Eusk. Sustainable developments sound great on paper, but it was a terrible business. A building built for sustainable living is only as good as it looks on paper - until the citizens reside in it. We are talking about having a room that could have its bed folded onto the wall with the living room and dining room combined into one. It may be sustainable but not worthy enough for VIPs. Charles looked at the clock, and it was about an hour away from the keynote speech by Roachie Wong. With some time left to spare, he wanted to explore the Shangri-Eusk. He knew the next time he walked into this magnificent building would be a distant future.

"Yo Charles, it's been a long time!" a familiar voice called out to Charles.

"Hey, John! Such a pleasant surprise. You attending the event as well?" Charles realized that the person calling him out was an old classmate.

However, what Charles did not expect to see was John wearing a uniform which gave him shivers down his spine. Where was it that Charles saw this uniform? He couldn't remember. Even his memories of having visited Gaia Facility for something were foggy. He tried and tried. To no avail, the sins he committed would not surface. All that remained was his instant fear and anxiety from seeing the uniform of Gaia Facility. To his horror, John was wearing the uniform of Gaia Facility.

"Did it mean that John is now a correction officer working in Gaia Facility?" Charles thought to himself. "No way! John has a big heart; there's no way he works for them. Right?"

"You ok there, Charles?" John looked at Charles with a puzzled look.

"Yes, I'm good. It's been so long. I see you're wearing the Gaia Facility uniform. I suppose you're working in there?"

"Oh yes, I am. I accepted my father's offer to join the Gaia

Facility as a Handler."

Father. A word not often heard in the era of smart cities. Parents consist of a father and a mother. With technological advancement and the way things were moving forward, the need for a pair of males and females was no longer needed to produce life. Pods and genetically modified babies were the things of the new era, but it was still a few years away from mass adoption. Most citizens in the smart cities didn't have families. It was taboo to speak of families as the citizens often came from one. It took guts and courage to leave their own families for the smart cities, which often left a bitter taste in their mouths.

"Why would my family not understand the need to fight climate change together?"

"Why would no one accept me for having no gender and being non-binary?"

"Why does everyone except me shun the idea of living in a smart city equipped with everything we humans need? Never needing to work another day in the hot sun. Never needing to get decimated by famines again!"

John was different from the citizens who moved to the smart cities. His family is of a certain nobility, hence the need for families. Families were a privilege for citizens from elite bloodlines. It was a tradition practiced by the nobilities of old and has remained untested. Joining the Gaia Facility wasn't as simple as having a spur-of-the-moment wish to aid in solving climate change - to John, it was something held in reverence: to represent his bloodline's best interest in being the rulers of society.

"Hey Charles, we should catch up sometime later. I have to go join my family in meeting my relatives."

"Yeah. We should catch up soon. How about…"

Before Charles could finish his sentence, armed guards of lesser rank from Gaia Facility surrounded John and escorted him. A sharp pain struck Charles as the image of armed guards started flashing in his head. "Where have I seen them before?" the mental trauma of his amnesiac experience in Gaia Facility left him wondering what happened that day.

The Sustain 4Ever Festival was finally underway. Each organization sent its best teams to each represent them for the presentation. Officials from smart cities and the old world attended the event. Some of the flags adorned by these officials were instantly recognizable to Charles. One thing that didn't sit well with Charles was how the smart cities and the old-world representatives interacted. As far as he could remember, weren't they at war with each other for their idealogy?

What happened to disliking each other and disassociating themselves in the name of "saving the earth"? Weren't the principles that the founding governing body set in stone for all citizens absolute and almighty? How can the governing body be conversing with the savages of the old world with such modesty? It seems they were playing catch-up after a long time. All this sustainability talk. The meatless future. The EVs. The Resla Rockets. The Supreme Being. Were the entire premise and founding philosophy of the cities just lies? Charles stared blankly at the officials, and when all hope seemed lost, a familiar voice - one that he instantly recognized from the binge-watching of keynote speeches from Sustain 4Ever festivals of old.

"Today is an important day in our lives. It is the Sustain 4Ever Festival. A festival held close to my heart as the day I became a made man."

Roachie Wong was on stage giving a speech. Charles could recognize him, but there was something amiss. The attire he was wearing. It was a tuxedo. The tuxedos were a banned dressing standard in smart cities in the name of equality; it was a sign of the old world where the capitalists would often put on for events.

"It is an honor for me to stand here before all of you as the keynote speaker of this event. Today we have a lineup of entrepreneurs ready to unveil their latest innovative offerings to the world."

Charles's head started to spin. "Entrepreneurs? Did I hear that correctly?" Charles looked around him and saw his fellow sustainapreneurs with the same confused look on their faces. Entrepreneurs were a dirty word; it was as good as throwing shade at a person. Entrepreneurship was often associated with the savages of the old world manipulating and taking advantage of their workers for profits. The sustainapreneurs were different; it was a progressive standard of innovation to serve the planet. What Charles could not understand was the sudden change in the demeanor of Roachie Wong. The last time he was still a sustainapreneur, now he was standing in front of him as an entrepreneur: complete tuxedo and all.

"To my esteemed guests representing their organizations and countries attending, thank you for gracing us with your presence. In our smart cities, we are eternally grateful for your contributions and guidance in forging the cities of tomorrow. Thank you, and to all fellow sustainapreneurs, I await you in the land of entrepreneurship!"

Like a bad nightmare, Charles wanted to wake up. Sustainapreneurs and entrepreneurs. Were they the same thing? How can it be? It was no use. Charles started to notice his fellow sustainapreneurs suddenly forgetting their creed. The anger in their eyes turned into admiration for Roachie Wong. The citizens from Lion's Hub went from being confused by Roachie's appearance to complete worship by his speech. It was a 180 in terms of behavior from them. The sustainapreneurs started to get riled up, and it was clear what was happening. They were ready to graduate from the crazy reality of sustainapreneurship to entrepreneurship. As easy as it took for them to assume an identity to assimilate into society, they were ready to shed this identity for a new one. That is what makes humans able to stand the test of time - our adaptability. The festival that Charles looked forward to attending started to turn into a disaster. Everything he worked for his entire life was a lie. The climate thing. The sustainability pledge. Everything became foggy to him. The ultimate sacrifice that citizens took upon themselves to leave everything behind from the old world in search of a utopia in the smart cities - was it all an illusion?

As Charles recalled the mental gymnastics he had to go through to give up eating meat to consume all that amount of bugs and soy to contribute toward a sustainable future, he started to have a violent reaction in his stomach. The memories of eating all that cockroaches and the plastic meat products swarmed his thoughts and made him sick. He wanted to throw up, but he couldn't. There was no way he could have a panic attack in public, especially when everyone was watching! Charles's head started to spin. He noticed his motions starting to look sloppy, and the microchip implanted in his arm began burning up. "Not yet. Not until!" summoning the resolve of a climate warrior, Charles pushed himself beyond his limits and stood his ground. The war is not lost yet. His turn to present the latest Plastic Meat for his organization was coming soon.

Taking to the stage was no easy task. Citizens before him presenting their products had stage fright. No surprises since the guests attending this festival were from the upper class of the smart cities and beyond (the not-so-savages of the old world". Having practiced the speech beforehand (and remembering the nagging voice of his boss in his ear), Charles gave perhaps the most convincing and impactful speech of the entire festival. The applause was aplenty, citizens were shocked at such a sustainable product, and even Roachie Wong was left speechless.

"Such beautiful spirit of entrepreneurship." a tear streamed down Roachie's cheek as he took the time to console himself, not wanting to look like an emotional mess in front of his fervent cult followers in the sustainapreneurs.

The ultimate battle was over. The spirit of sustainapreneurship was truly alive in the hearts of Charles. He believed in the mission and goal of his product. Now the time has arrived for him to achieve immortality like Roachie Wong and the Supreme Being. Expecting the whole smart city to cower beneath his feet and worshipped the grounds he walked on, Charles looked around the festival halls for signs of life. However, no one seemed to bat an eye at Charles. Citizens and enthusiasts didn't care about Charles's presentation. Neither did they bother with his Plastic Meat fallacy. These sheep attended the festival for a feel-good moment. A moment of virtue signaling - to pledge their allegiance to the cause of sustainability. No one truly cared. One presentation starts? Let's cue the applause. Oh, the presentation has ended? Let's have the applause again.

The only thing that mattered to these citizens was to do the right thing most of the time, ignoring the reality and consequences of their actions. For as long as they can live a life of decadence in the towering metropolis of the smart cities, not needing to have a single ounce of sweat dropped by being productive, so be it. Even in the name of giving up their liberty and bodily autonomy: of what it means to be human, it was a price they were willing to pay. Just because they supported sustainability doesn't mean they were bothered about it. In the streets of Lion's Hub, the citizens weren't responsible for the upkeep of it. The citizens truly lived lives of ignorance - just like a cog of the machine in the madness of a technological utopia. A social experiment worthy of being commemorated in the Guinness book of records.

"Yo Charles, what a great presentation from you. That idea of yours? Amazing." when all hope seemed lost, John appeared.

"Thanks, John, it means a lot to me."

"What's with the sour look on your face? Hey, my father told me to invite you to join us. You free later on?"

"Yes, I am. Where would we meet later?"

"Oh, you just take the lift to the upper levels. See u in abit, Broski!"

Broski. A word often used in the old world where close friends would call one another. Since Charles moved into Lion's Hub, no one has ever called him by that. Citizen was what was used by everyone. Their names had no significance anymore. Even when John called out to him with his name Charles, there was a sense of nostalgia. The last time someone called him by his name was when he was a savage from the old world. That feeling stung like a wasp. It was so long since he got acknowledged as a human.

Clenching his fists, the illusion of the utopia started to fade.

Charles knew what he needed to do next. It was time for a date with destiny.

The Unveiling

With each step Charles took, he could feel the shackles coming off. A heart once filled with purpose now became one filled with understanding. "Was this the ultimate goal of it all?": it was an epiphany Charles finally reached, with several of his predecessors before him who got it having the same thought.

Charles was easily towering over everyone else from the lift's view. Standing perched on the mountain of omnipotence, Charles felt a sense of power and steadfastness. Never once in his life has he had this kind of feeling; it felt kind of surreal. He was always wanting to be part of the crowd. The drive to create solutions in the name of saving the earth. All the things he swore to give up and the new values he embraced, all in the name of accomplishing his life's goal. His goal of finally reaching Roachie is complete, and what's left for him is to move forward.

"Ding Dong!" the lift has reached its destination.

"Good Afternoon Mr, may I know your name?"

"Charles, from Meatless to Meat. Citizen of Lion's Hub."

"Greetings. We welcome you to the Shangri-La Club. We hope you have a pleasant experience."

A professionally dressed gentleman greeted Charles. The attire he wore was one of the old world, adorned by hotel staff. Being greeted by a human before entering a building, even a room, was not something Charles expected. The smart cities were manned autonomously by AI and humanoid robots, citing the need to reduce the greenhouse and carbon emissions by a human; there was no longer a need for humans to have these kinds of climate-destructive jobs. Charles finally understood this climate rally nonsense: these were mere propaganda slurs to convince the citizens to live the way the controllers desired. Charles was selected to join the controllers of society, far higher than the levels that the cult members of the governing body could ever reach. With an air of pedigree, Charles made his rounds in the club.

The club was the most beautiful and architecturally designed floor Charles had ever seen. The marble on the walls, the slick carpet with historically rich patterns, and the guests in it made the entire room feel important. A lumpy feeling thumped in Charles's chest as he caught the glances of humans of the opposite sex glancing at him. That feeling was something he could not comprehend. In his entire existence in Lion's Hub, females were just a construct. A gender. Nothing more than that. Humans of the opposite sex.

These females were not just the run-of-the-mill mass-produced factory females that Lion's Hub has. Their dresses accentuated their gender's best features. Their faces are enhanced by what appears to be powder - bringing out the radiance and life that only a female can create - and their bodies have a piece of fabric hugging their curvy body. Charles could not believe that females could look this good. His eyes seemed to be failing him as he wondered if this was just a dream.

The women glancing at Charles chuckled; perhaps they understood Charles, hence his weird mannerisms. Charles did not know what to do; was he going to stand there like a whiney little citizen, or was he going to do what savages of the old world do - and approach these ladies to introduce himself?

"Good evening! My name is Citizen Charles of Lion's Hub. A pleasure to meet you females." upon finishing his sentence, Charles realized his mistake. Females? Citizen? His face was flustered, and the ladies across him noticed it; they couldn't help but contain their laughter.

"Good evening Charles, my name is Laura. These are my two sisters, Lorraine and Lydia. Unlike you, we aren't citizens." Laura gestured to her two sisters.

Trying to find the words to describe where they came from, Laura was thinking of the best way to talk to Charles. Saying "from the old world" might elicit a strange response, considering that Charles looks to be a brand new chosen one from this batch of sustainapreneurs. After much pondering, Laura decided to go along with the name of the country she resided.

"We are from Germany. Close to the Euro Hub. A pleasure to meet you.", Laura continued, unsure if Charles even knew where Germany was. The version of history taught in the cities differed from the kind of history the "savages" like her knew.

"Germany… Is that part of the old world?"

"Yes, it is."

"That must mean."

"Yes, I am a so-called savage, as you citizens know. Besides, is this how you citizens all talk? So prim and proper?"

"Wh-what!!"

Laura and her sisters could not help but laugh at Charles's red face and contorted demeanor. They tried hard to contain their laughter at Charles out of respect for a brand-new citizen shedding his skin to become a controller. The sudden paradigm shift was taking a toll on Charles's mental capacity.

"You know what, Charles, see you in a bit. It seems that dinner is starting soon." Laura knew the fun had just started as she recalled that citizens don't eat meat. She knew Charles was in for a rude awakening.

Briskly walking away with her sisters, Laura turned around and winked at Charles, blowing a kiss at him, leaving Charles dumbfounded. Never has a female ever charmed the daylights out of him. "He is definitely in for a treat when he sees what's for dinner.", Laura thought to herself as a group of men approached her from a distance, eager to impress her.

A group of hotel staff appeared and ushered the esteemed guests to the dining hall. Anxiety filled Charles as he realized what was going to happen. There might be a chance that they served real meat, the bane of everything he stood for and swore his entire existence to destroy. He knew his actions and behavior in the Shangri-La Club were making him stand out - an uncharacteristic behavior, almost like a savage - Charles reached an epiphany, and his face turned white from his sudden realization.

"Did the savages of the old world view us, citizens, as the real savages?"

The color drained from Charles's face as he followed the hotel staff's direction when ushering the guests. For the longest time, he thought he was the most civilized being, evolved from the savagery plaguing the world from a net-zero future. He could see laughter, chatter, and the guests alongside him (they were no longer savages but his friends!) all seemed to be having a good time. This unity was unseen and unheard of in the cities. Most citizens would seem to be tolerating one another in the name of climate change, but other than that common goal: there wasn't anything else that could glue them. These guests were different. They didn't believe in climate change. They didn't believe in giving up their bodily functions by implanting a microchip in them. There was a sense of kindred and friendship. Something Charles craved for the longest time. A belief and understanding that would propel him forward, not one of pure desire - an artificial belief system pumped out by the governing body to assimilate the citizens into a shared future decided by someone else.

"Charles, come join me later!"

It was John, and he spotted Charles from a distance. More like John has been up to date with everything Charles has been doing and even assigned a special strike force to accompany him for this mission. Ever since Charles took up his offer and entered the Shangri-La Club, the Gaia Facility officers in John's platoon have been eyeing Charles. They wanted to monitor Charles's every action to ensure he goes crazy over the "unplugging" sequence.

Unplugging from the Grid

The "unplugging" sequence: interestingly enough, it was the terminology used by the Gaia Facility to safely un-assimilate a potential citizen from the madness of the smart cities. The goal of smart cities was to divide the world into different zones. Since Charles broke the pledge some time ago, he has been added to the list of "important" citizens to monitor. Most citizens would never dare to go against the citizen's pledge, as most feared being kicked out and banished back to the old world. Showing the potential to one day become a controller of the world, the Gaia Facility had allowed him to prove himself. Having your solitary thought and coming up with your decision-making process has become an afterthought in cities. The microchip implanted - solved most of the problems the citizens had. The microchip not only transcended the humans into citizens of the smart cities, but it could also read the vitals, monitor the brain waves, and allow connection to Harry AI. Harry AI knows all, and Harry AI can indirectly influence the very thought of each citizen. By sending signals to the citizens, Harri AI could make citizens angry, sad, happy, emotional, and serious, to name a few, anytime it wishes.

"Charles, the time has finally come for you to join us. All your sacrifices. Everything was all for this moment."

John recalled the times when people laughed at Charles during college. Being a savage from the old world meant he had a different motivation from the other second-generation citizens. John didn't bother with any criticisms Charles received; he knew deep down that every citizen had a chance to become a controller. John could see the resolve in Charles's eyes from day one.

Charles had a myriad of odd-looking things in front of him. The idea of having all these types of meat was foreign to him. "Whatever happened to the ban on meat and "no livestock killed" anymore?" Charles remembered the lies Lion's Hub has been feeding the citizens even till now. Charles sighed as he concluded an hour ago that everything he knew before this moment was a pipe dream. The inversion is the truth.

"Come on, the moment of truth!"

John and his team of Gaia Facility officers were spying on Charles from a distance. They were as excited as a bunch of children playing at the playground for the first time. Charles and his plate filled with all kinds of delectable foods seemed ready to embark on a brand new expedition towards his awakening.

The Sheep becomes the Shepherd

Charles's heart was thumping like crazy. A whirlwind of a day. First, it started with him attending the Sustain 4Ever festival. Then he realized that one cared about his product launches and treated him like a brand new circus monkey. Then, his eyes laid on some of the most beautiful, stunning, and gorgeous women ever. Fast forward to now, his hands were carrying a plate of what was supposed to be a cardinal sin - as bad as a war criminal carrying out atrocities - meat, seafood, and heck, even a glass of red wine.

"Where should I begin?"

Charles grabbed a piece of the chicken and hesitated to take a bite. What if this entire Shangri-La Club was another ruse to throw him into the Gaia Facility again? However, that chicken was glistening in the light due to its seasoning and decor; the Roachie Bot 3.3 must have done something to make it look this good. Mentally correcting himself, there was no Roachie Bot 3.3 preparing the food here; it was all cooked and plated by a team of Chefs. A meal prepared by a Chef was the first time for Charles. That was enough justification for him to take a big bite of that piece of chicken! To hell with the Plastic Meat!

"...!...!...! De-delicious!"

As soon as Charles took a big bite of the chicken, he could feel his senses overridden by its taste profile. The years spent conditioned to consume synthetic meat came undone; the real meat he just consumed cured him of his nightmare. Like a fleeting memory, the experience of eating synthetic trash went into the deep recesses of his brain. Two big bites later, Charles finished his entire plate.

"Wow, this is so good."

"Such smooth taste… I must get myself more!"

Charles could not help himself; it became an experience he didn't want to end. If freedom tasted this good, he didn't want to give up on it. Years of suffering and being brainwashed were over. He has finally reached the pinnacle of life. Savages of the old world? Just a slur by the citizens who didn't want to take ownership of their own lives.

"Let's roll." John has seen enough and signaled to his team of Gaia Facility officers to carry on with the mission. John prepared himself by ensuring his uniform looked as fresh as possible.

"Hey Charles, how was the meal?"

"…"

"Hey Charles, can you hear me?"

"…"

Charles was too engrossed with gorging himself with meat after meat. There was no stopping his overindulgence. In his mind, the only way to move forward was to embrace the values he gave up on when he became a citizen of Lion's Hub. To become an entrepreneur like Roachie Wong, he had to embody the essence of being human. That is to live, enjoy and love. The savages of the old world had the right thing going on for the longest time. The Sustain 4Ever festival changed everything that day for the trajectory of Charles's life.

John was pleased with what he saw. The reports he read, and the preparation his team has done. It leads to this moment - when a citizen has reached a score to become part of the team - a controller of the smart cities. Everything he saw Charles committing - the gorging of meat, the desire for beautiful women, the drive to attain power - was just as planned.

"Hey Charles, I have someplace to bring you. There are some important people here in attendance. I would like to introduce you to them."

Charles looked up and finally noticed John.

"Sorry, I was having too much of a time eating." Charles wiped his mouth with a piece of tissue before continuing. "Sure, let's do that!"

Charles knew deep down he was above everyone else. To foolishly think he was beneath those dumb citizens in smart cities? Impossible. Most people would second-guess themselves and run away from such an opportunity to meet with important people. But not him; whatever it takes to achieve his goals, he would do it.

Charles has a brand new purpose in life. He stood tall with his shoulders straightened and walked with a degree of omnipotence.

"It is time for me to rule over these citizens." Charles gave a devilish smirk as he recalled.

"Power corrupts, and absolute power corrupts absolutely."

Chapter 7: The Winning Play for the Future

On May 8th, 2020, a trial was conducted by the Singaporean government at Singapore's Bishan-Ang Mo Kio Park. With the cause of "promoting safe distancing measures" to curb the spread of Covid-19, the masses saw the robodogs for the first time. Who built these robodogs? It was none other than everyone's favorite: Boston Dynamics.

Yes, Boston Dynamics, the same company that inspired one of the episodes of Black Mirror. There was a mixed reaction regarding the unveiling of robodogs to the public. It ranged from children being fascinated by these mechanical dogs; to "tech gurus" having all kinds of pie-in-the-sky orgasmic reactions to a soon-to-be reality of mechas and robots and made some adults question the existence of robots patrolling.

The elephant in the room is neither of those realizations. The biggest thing regarding that robot is that, in reality, it existed years ago - all it takes is some catastrophic event for the ones behind them to unveil them to the public. As a child, I've always questioned everything. Questioning everything as it seems in this current climate of censorship, mass cancellation, conformity, and the assimilation of the individual into the group instead of coming to your conclusions - is a dangerous thing or a personality trait. The book I read was called "The Future is faster than you think," a book written by tech entrepreneurs. It highlights that emerging & disruptive technologies are being created and can come to the mass market faster than most expect. It also described how these technologies could potentially change our lives, enhancing them and making the human experience easier.

Adversity changes a man for the better. A man who has not experienced hardship cannot be called a man. Nothing shapes a man more than the battles he has fought, the strife in their life, the setbacks, the journey, and so much more. Walking the streets of Singapore, I see a generation of lost souls assimilated into groupthink. Growing up in the era of social media tools like TikTok and Instagram has led them to develop identities synonymous with one another. Thankfully, my generation didn't grow up with these tools; they came about as I was in my teens, and smartphones back then weren't as immersive and privacy-killing as they are now.

When technology makes life progressively easier, adversity in a human's life is lost. What seems to be adversity has become eradicated by the fragility of the youth's mental state. Every single problem that these youths face has a term, even down to their gender, which somehow is a problem today. The need for inclusivity and acceptance of everything has forced the individual to embrace the group's identity. Going against the group would lead to personal and financial ruin for many.

As these technologies presented to the world eventually go mainstream, I could only imagine how meaningless human existence will inevitably become. To be human is to live life to its fullest. To try and fail and get up and try again. With tools like Google existing, nobody will go through the whole notion of failing; a simple Google search on a topic would lead to an instant instruction manual on how to get the thing done - all without going through the trial and error phase. Imagine when these "disruptive" technologies arrive; how more so would humanity descend into when there would be no more troubles, just a life filled with social activities that the central planners in each country have deemed fit for recreational use?

The Covid-19 incident, with its lockdowns and impact, has further divided humanity into different fragmented shards. On one side, we have the pro-lockdown crowd who embraces the rule of the Big

Brother government to protect them from death from Covid-19. On the other hand, we have the liberty bunch who vouched for their sovereign rights as human beings to go wherever they wish, not allowing the government to infringe on their rights. This divide between humanity became segmented by the mask mandate, the vaccine mandates, the social distancing, and all that crazy new mandates socially engineered to see how far humans will comply.

The next big segway due to Covid-19 restrictions is the engineering collapse of the energy markets. With the Ukraine-Russia conflict blamed as the boogieman responsible for the lack of gas, fertilizers, and whatnot, the whole world once again shifted its collective attention towards the authoritarian rule of President Vladimir Putin. The truth was, Putin's ban on exports was just the tip of the iceberg; the lack of commodities was the Covid-19 restrictions which led to a drop in demand and workers. When things kicked back into high gear almost overnight, there was a lack of supply to meet demand.

The effects of social unrest due to the lack of trust in governments, in part to their response to Covid-19, led to massive riots and worldwide protests. There were underlying issues before the pandemic, but it was slowly built up over time to erupt into anger and resentment against their oppressors, the government - which was supposed to be working for the power, not against it.

Currencies started to see their value dwindle due to the lack of purchasing power. Money printing due to stimulus checks, debasement of different currencies, and even the sudden boom in the strength of the U.S. dollar, the world reserve currency, led to the global currency issue. Humanity saw their life-long savings worth less every second and became anxious and agitated. My experience of being in Turkey, way before the rest of the world opened up, gave me a first-hand experience of crazy sky-high inflation where prices went up nearly every day. Imagine living in that country with a fixed wage, and prices keep rising.

World Economic Forum

One of the topics discussed amongst the pro-liberty group is the existence of a specific NGO (non-governmental organization) known as the World Economic Forum (WEF). Many videos and articles are written extensively regarding the policies and goals that this NGO wishes to achieve. From overreaching and entirely "disruptive" goals like having a future of synthetic meat to a reality where people will "own nothing and be happy." It seems a little outlandish and odd that an NGO can come out of nowhere and proclaim such provocative statements.

However, what seems to be nothing more than just outlandish plots straight out of a James Bond movie becomes eerily sinister when you start to see the WEF's goals become materialized. With their members being ministers from countries all over the world and some being key appointment holders in some big organizations, I can't help but notice a systematic "great reset" taking place in real-time. There were fiat currency problems, famines, food shortages, the brand new psyche and belief systems youths have, and even the Covid-19 restrictions. All these things that appear unconnected have seemingly formed an interconnected web where they are all connected.

Scrolling the web page of the WEF, I can't help but try to navigate the page to see if this NGO has any members represented by Singaporeans. Not to my shock, a group of Singaporeans is part of the WEF. It ranged from having professions and positions of leadership in some companies/start-ups that I've never seen nor heard of in recent years. This revelation raised a particular red flag in me - the WEF Singaporeans will be involved with some plan or goal they want to achieve. Who knows, it may have already begun.

The Hive Mind calls

The link between the fall of the hawker scene making way for a business haven in Singapore interconnected. Once a country makes way for a plan focusing on international people coming and doing business here, it loses its identity. I have tried to look for expatriates who enjoy our local food, going to different hawker centers, and even having a plate of Char Kway Teow. None of them entertain the thought of stepping into a hawker center. With an expert-level salary package, leasing a condo with amazing views, and an unlimited amount of googly-eyed Singaporean women on tap at a swipe on their dating app - these are the only things they love about Singapore.

Almost all these expatriates bring the skills and "experience" - whatever experience is - sitting in a cubicle and attending useless meetings for years counts as that in the corporate world. It almost entirely revolves around tech, healthcare, and finance. The tech industry in Singapore has made expatriates pursue it. The truth is that this salary package isn't "real." It's all due to the crazy money printing leading to the stock market going up artificially. These tech companies, having their valuation inflated and pumped crazily, have the budget to hire these workers by waving these crazy packages. But there is more to it than the crazy packages; not every tech worker knows what they are doing. There is a saying: "The real techies are in FAANG." FAANG stands for Facebook, Apple, Amazon, Netflix, and Google. A prediction I made long ago is that all the people in the world are required to funnel into the tech industry. When people start to see these socially engineered demands for tech workers and the salary packages offered, the youths are inclined to take the bait. Giving up their dreams and aspirations, they take up many ridiculous roles such as front-end whatever (software engineers in the past used to do everything) to have a slice of this fake, synthetic pie.

So, what is the end game? Just a bunch of people working in tech? Yes and no. The primary outcome of this tech push for everyone to become involved with a desk-bound job is to condition the next generation of the human race that value gets derived from the number of currency units you have.

With each moment humans spend their time at a desk, they get desensitized from the real world. Who is going to spend time on that oil rig? How about laying those bricks for real estate? This problem is getting progressively worse when most people's pivotal moment in their lives is bragging about earning a big salary package and having a staff canteen that provides world-class food for them for free.

A simple explanation and example of desensitization from the real world? The food delivery experiment. The future youths will never know how food is made, from farm to table. They don't go to hawker centers and see the food cooked in real-time. It comes from a tap on the screen, some digital transaction where their digits go down, and the food arrives sometime later. TLDR - food comes from tapping on screens.

Then again, it isn't just that easy for people to willingly float towards the tech industry just for a big salary. Some people aren't motivated simply by having more currency units, hence the need for a rallying cry - a new artificial movement for more people to assimilate into the hive mind.

Climate Change

During my days in the public school education system, the term "climate change" wasn't thrown around that much It was often associated with "global warming," with "climate change" being the new name christened. There was a movement for the "3Rs" which meant: recycling, reusing, and reducing. Recycling bins appeared next to garbage bins in my secondary school, but nobody paid attention to them. Despite the brightly blue-colored recycling bin being there, it failed to garner my classmate's attention.

Humans tend to go for the easier option every time, hence the appeal for technology to transform the human experience from learning to optimization. The smartwatch has replaced the casual watch people wear, and businesses like Swatch and those customizable mid-tier watch shops have gone out of business. The Apple Watch has disrupted (for lack of a better word) the game. Walk around the CBD of any first-world country, and nearly everywhere worker owns one. The Apple Watch can not only tell the time but can be used with Apply Pay to make payments (such as transport and their overpriced morning Starbucks Coffee) and even be used as a pseudo-phone.

So that begs the question: "How do we go about Climate Change as the recycling bin system didn't work?"

One can simply put themselves into the shoes of our beloved central planners at the WEF. With many of their goals being sustainable this and sustainable that. Just like the education system is the gateway for many youths to broaden their minds - one tweak was all it took to make this climate change a part of their lives. The inclusion of climate change was the next big step in the grand scheme. My parent's generation didn't give two hoops about climate change; there were more concerned with their own lives. Understandably so, Singapore didn't have many opportunities back then. The quality of life wasn't as it is now. With each generation being born, their perception of reality changes as much. Mine had climate change introduced, but it was a feeble effort.

The simple act of making the term climate change exist in our subconscious mind is more important to the central planners than making it a widespread phenomenon within one generation's lifetime. Remember this - the central planner's aim and goals have spanned over thousands of years, and if one were to be a betting man on their patience - I wouldn't suggest betting against them. With my generation being exposed to climate change and eventually growing up to become cogs in the machine, some would find themselves in academia and public office. Initially, these starry-eyed workers wouldn't believe in climate change. However, most people have no backbone. If you want to buy a person's heart, just dangle money in front of their face. Morals and respect for themselves go out the window in the face of financial incentives. Since there is an incentive to support anything that pays them well, these people in academia and public office would do anything.

Like the chapter before, let's call these people (I shall give no pronouns, as they usually fall into the same wokester mentality) the citizens.

These citizens would teach the next generation and become agents of the new climate change regime and demand for change. Some of these citizens would have children. The cycle will then carry on. The new generation would become immersed in climate change. I can easily see this change in real-time. Let's talk about another completely different industry - esports. The idea of having your children sitting in front of a screen and playing video games would be ludicrous - if I suggested this to you two decades ago. Fast forward to today, the idea of being an esports athlete, spending years of your life glued to their black mirror, has become normalized. Why? Because these games of old have grown up and have started their own families. It is acceptable in society to be a gamer in the 2020s.

I remember having a meetup with youths ten years younger than I am. The usual banter and introductions occurred as we got to know each other. Suddenly the topic changed to climate change as we were talking about Covid-19. They mentioned how clean the streets and the air have become due to the Covid-19 lockdown. "In the name of saving the planet and solving climate change, lockdowns are good. We can save the planet by going out and consuming less." That was one of the sentences my friend said that sent chills down my spine.

The idea of climate lockdowns was not a fantasy theorized by professors and researchers. It's a real thing that will come sometime down the road. It's shocking how far this climate change has seeped into our reality. The youths of today are all fervent supporters of this movement, and in turn, the reality we live in has become one where the rallying cry is one of climate change. Taking a walk around Singapore, I see "green movements" starting in our public transportation system. Posters of how we "should track our carbon footprint" based on our transport habits are one example.

Another big one is the mobile banking app, the DBS Mobile app. Now, when I make my monthly credit card bill, there's a new tab that shows "carbon footprint." It tells me the purchases I have charged to my card and the amount of carbon footprint emitted. Wow, such amazing innovation. Give that Mobile App Engineer a raise, please.

It's as though the entire climate change thing has evolved from the stage of awareness to a full-blown religion. Resla became the darling of climate change advocates, and its founder Elon Musk (The Supreme Being), has become a star in today's mainstream culture. Taking a page out from "How not to be Tech Founder," Elon Musk has created a cult of personality for himself. Doing the exact opposite his predecessors have done, he went full-on with his exposure to popular culture by appearing on the Joe Rogan Show. Lighting up his cigar, Elon immediately got exposure to the mainstream audience, and everyone adored him for that.

Most recently, Elon has also gotten himself involved with the cryptocurrency crowd by becoming an advocate for "freedom." With strategic timing, he became the face of this industry by popularizing the meme cryptocurrency coin, Dogecoin, and Shiba Inu. With a tweet from his phone, Elon could effectively control the price action of these meme coins. For many, it was a golden opportunity to "get rich quick," and the ever-contrarian crowd of renowned investors could see through his act. Further on, Elon added Bitcoin to his company's balance sheet and even made headlines by planning on allowing Dogecoin as a currency for purchasing a Resla.

Think about this, a cryptocurrency project used for speculation finally has a use case. However, looking past all the hype and the irrelevant stock price of Tesla. One group of people has done the ultimate work - research on EVs.

Many research and resources online have been talking about EVs and their components. The truth about EVs is that you cannot build one without raw materials and natural resources. Some videos deep-dived into the materials and stressed how these resources would deplete due to rising demand. However, mining these resources and bringing them to the mass market for production would also cause climate change due to the amount of oil, gas, and the rest needed.

The same industry that the climate warriors swore to destroy - the Oil & Gas, Mining, and Natural Resources - is the same enemy that is needed to fulfill the dreams of these dumb idealists. This scenario has become a Catch-22, as you can't build your net-zero reality without raw materials and the oil that powers it up - how about the smart cities that could solve their pipe dream of a so-called "sustainable future"? The same industry demonized is needed as well!

With the kind of mental gymnastics in the collective minds of these citizens, they could only theorize about using artificial intelligence, 3D printing, and other forms of "innovations" to go about their sustainable dream. This goal is unachievable since these climate warriors have zero experience in the real world. The only way for them is to become associated by kowtowing to their masters in the political and financial elite to carry out their work in the ESG/climate area.

The amount of legal tender notes siphoned by the hands of

private citizens through taxation and insane money printing has become an endless reserve that governments could use to reallocate this money to their agencies and politically connected organizations in the private sector. Who is to blame? The government is simply answering the cry of their woke citizens who demand green everything!

That's a big reason governments and their central planners have been trying to clamp down on the rich. The rich people aren't on the same team. They control resources and equity that the controllers cannot reach, from offshore trusts, private property, vaults of gold & silver, paper currency, and private companies structured to protect themselves. The rich have positioned themselves to avoid them facing the wrath of the hand of their government.

With cash-losing adoption, QR Codes are being normalized everywhere, with their origins in China. The next step is to usher in the era of CBDC (Central Bank Digital Currency). Once in place, the everyday Joe is forced to accept this new currency else they can't put the bread on the table. The blockchain system the freedom group loves will become the same rope the central planners will use to hang them.

Of course, climate change is the ultimate goal. Equality and social cohesion are part of the pipeline too. There is a common enemy that these citizens have.

I want you to win!

And this enemy is you! To pick up this book and read it. Kudos to you. You probably heard about me from somewhere. An acquaintance from my Yu-Gi-Oh! Days? Perhaps you followed me throughout my card game history? Maybe you heard about me from my podcast? There's also an odd chance that you know me in real life.

The enemy is the sovereign individual. The sovereign seeks to safeguard their livelihoods from the utopia the central planners have planned for ages.

The goal of climate change, from my perspective, isn't so much of making everyone eat bugs and live in pods, being microchipped, and being tracked everywhere you go. The true purpose is to give humanity a common goal, purpose, and reason for living. To replace the subconscious psyche based on the whims of the central planners, they have succeeded in it multiple times throughout history. And the end game: an eternity of slavery in a technological dystopia where you will own nothing and be happy.

This planned future for smart cities with governments hyping the need for sustainable development. As a former Software Engineer, I know how these cities work and how lethal they can be to a sovereign individual. Imagine every move you make getting recorded instantaneously into an immutable blockchain. Not that tracking isn't new to us; the smartphone tied to our bodies has become a symbiotic relationship. The next step of the goals to be achieved by our tech overlords will be the microchip that will somehow become implanted into our arms. Society has embraced the goals of the central planners/the elite gradually. The Covid-19 pandemic has lifted the veil on everyone's eyes on many, including mine. It showed me how society's conditioning is to live in fear. When did this massive fear campaign start? It's as tough a question as how we start to dislike our fellow humans. Everything starts from the day we first step into the public school education system; our minds become warped, molded into perfect cogs to perform our needed functions in society.

With each step we take in our lives, humans become more pragmatic. The goals and dreams we once had have been suppressed and dumbed down by the needs of the collective. The "sustainable dream" of going net-zero, plant-based, no more meat, and all that has replaced the dreams of many. It has become astounding to me when I sit down with people younger than me, and most of their aspirations are only in the form of a career such as a lawyer, a doctor, an engineer, and worst of all - to join the tech industry. No human born will ever want to have a career as their dream; it's a socially engineered phenomenon that has seeped into our culture.

You, the reader, might think: "It sure sounds damn gloomy from here on out; what can I do to survive in this future of a tech dystopia." There are some things within your reach, and there are some that are not. The more time spent thinking of impossible scenarios would eventually lead to mental burnout and a lack of discipline to focus on doing the tasks at hand to secure a better future for you, your family, and the children you will have in the future.

The west, be it in the USA or some of the more western countries in the EU (European Union), doesn't look like the best place to live in the 21st century. There were times I thought about going to Europe, but the intel I've received has made me think twice about it. Famines, food shortages, energy crises, civil unrest, and much more are some reasons to justify my decision to hold off on my expedition.

I truly believe being born in Singapore before the peak of my nation's prosperity is the greatest blessing in disguise. Imagine if I was raised in some random corner in Eastern Europe or some slum in a liberal state in the US - the opportunities presented to me wouldn't be available. Also, being born to a family of skilled professionals and growing up in an estate with entrepreneurs and hardworking men have instilled in me a degree of discipline and worldview that is uncommon among the current generation of Singaporeans. Having traveled abroad many times, I've also seen many countries and always counted my blessing upon having my feet touch Singaporean soil upon returning. There is truly no place like home.

Of course, there are some things you cannot control. There was no way I could control where I was born and my family. The generation before me made these decisions - my parents - and the environment they chose to have me in. You also cannot people, the crazy masses, the people who do not seem to align with the same views you have. That is understandably so - if everyone believes in the same thing, it would ultimately lead to a hive mind kind of scenario: the climate change narrative playing right in front of our eyes. The more people have tried to control how people think, the less they understand what it means to be human.

Once you get past the stage of trying to change the world to your whim, realize that our experience on this planet is fleeting and temporary. A feeling of serenity and calm will fill your soul. One needs to understand that happiness, sadness, and a whole variety of emotions cannot dictate the flow of your life. Your existence on this planet is the same as everyone else; it is up to you to live the life you want. The goal is to live intentionally. Let's start with the factors you can control.

Control of your financials

I've known many people who stress about not making too much money, not having enough money to do the things they want, and not being able to spend and enjoy life. It's the same thoughts over and over again. Some people make over 6-digits a year and complain they can't enjoy their lives.

Depending on your income and profession, money is never enough. The reason isn't that stuff costs too much, or the prices of everything keep going up. It certainly isn't because retirement is an impossible pipe dream. Money is infinite, and as long as a central bank exists in your nation in charge of the currency units, money will never be enough for anyone. With a swift keyboard stroke, the money printer can fire up and inject new currency units into the system. At another moment, it can change into a money vacuum and suck back the circulating money supply.

For the longest time, I sat down and wrote down financial plans on how much money I needed to retire comfortably and do nothing. That was me during the two years spent working in a corporate job. I'm glad I am no longer that person anymore. With the events of the stimulus checks and the crazy inflation everywhere in sight, the ability for a person to become "financially independent" has become another carrot on the stick scenario. I understand that some find solace in working a corporate job, and being an entrepreneur isn't for everyone. I know some who have side hustles while working their corporate 9-5.

What I learned so far is that starting a business and running it - the joy and satisfaction from it far outweigh everything being an employee can ever provide you. My father's advice to work first before starting a business made me see things from both perspectives. The difference between getting a wage and paying yourself accordingly to the profits left over after the overhead is like night and day.

Life has become much more enjoyable with mental and physical strength after getting on the path of entrepreneurship. I now spend my mornings reading and walking outside, watching the sunrise on my face, and being grateful for being alive. I exercise twice daily and am proud to look in my absolute best physical form. These are the things that money can't buy - your health and your mental state.

One of the goals of financial control in your life is to achieve a healthy mental state and the peak physical shape you can be. Everything else past that point is a surplus. Apart from your mental and health status, the next goal of financial control is a more practical one - having multiple bank accounts, your profession, and your business. Multiple bank accounts can protect you from the scenario where one country decides to block your transactions from it. Some countries allow you to open one with a tourist visa, while some require residence permits. A profession can be incredibly versatile; the best is to have a location-independent one, and some examples are software development, writing, content creation, and digital marketing.

As for business, this is a tricky one. Most countries are starting to implement a flat 15% "common corporate tax rate." We all know the benefits of Dubai and its 0% taxes - that begs the question - for how long more? Georgia also has a business tax rate of 1%, but it is a geographically remote location far away for most people, and many airlines don't have direct flights to that country. Digital Nomad Visas are also getting incredibly easy to apply for, with their requirements getting easier to fulfill. The location of your business can be anywhere if the products and services offered are location-independent.

There's an argument for blockchain technology - mainly the one the freedom maxis love to rave about all day - the need for decentralized technology and the usage of Bitcoin. Many believe in the potential of Bitcoin and how it can change the world of cross-border payments, getting rid of the big banks and their scummy ways. With the latest developments of all these blockchain companies and their implosion with the recent rate hike, I still am a contrarian believer that blockchain is here to stay. However, whether this decentralized movement is good for society as a whole - I leave this up to you to decide - it does feel good to have some Bitcoin stored in a hardware wallet as an alternative currency.

Gold & Silver. My mother has a friend who is always big on gold. The friend loves gold so much that he seems to be the only way actively buying and holding them since two decades ago. The reason why he does that? "Money isn't real, so any excess I have goes into gold." My mother would often shrug him off respectfully since everyone has their own opinion. My gold journey kickstarted my interest in commodities and natural resources. The book "Hot Commodities" by legendary investor Jim Rogers made me realize that most financial gurus who made a career out of the artificially inflated stock market have no absolute clue about how the economy works. I think holding gold doesn't do much for the average person; it is only beneficial if you have some sort of paper wealth. You can either keep gold on your own (at home) or in a vault. One website I use to purchase gold is Bullion Star, a gold company based in Singapore.

I also cannot stress how comparing yourself with others is detrimental to controlling your financial outlook. Especially with this era of social media, it gets to everyone's head how they should live a life that is supposed to look "successful" and "rich." I have acquaintances who constantly stalk and comment on the lifestyle I portray on Instagram, with the meals, the travels (which are business travels), and the experiences. Instead of wanting to be like me, they can choose to unplug Instagram and live their individual lives.

Everyone's ideal lifestyle is different, some may optimize their life to have a cup of latte every morning, and some have theirs to include non-stop travels to new countries. Some wish to stay home and waste their lives playing video games all day. You need to unplug from social media and live life on your terms. Remember this - social media is nothing more than a highlight reel of a person's life.

Once you have achieved all of these steps, financial control over your life will be nearly complete; until the CBDC system gets rolled out and the financial end game has arrived for most of us.

Control of your environment

Your parents had no control over where they were born. However, when they decided to get married and have you - they finally had control over where they chose to live and have a family. That's the same control over the environment as an individual - where you choose to live.

That's the same amount of control you have. I placed it after controlling your financials because, without some level of wealth, you will not be able to manipulate your environment. The term expatriate has a terrible reputation. In Singapore, the term means the caucasian guy working in Singapore, often paired with a young local Singaporean girl. Somehow almost every female acquaintance I know has either had or wants to go out with these "ang moh" or white men. So there is some truth to it. Nothing makes a local more interested in someone than them being from abroad.

It isn't common knowledge that the number one motivator for men to move abroad and achieve some level of financial control is to increase their value in society. In a first-world country, having a lot of money combined with assets means a higher status for men. Moving abroad for work for a man means that his skillset is valued overseas, and in doing so, would raise his overall value. I'm a believer in traveling and experiencing different cultures and economies. Having traveled to more than two dozen countries in my youth, my peers would often engage me and ask about what life is like overseas.

Imagine if it were you, a man has had the chance to work abroad. Preferably having worked in more than two countries in your lives, the wealth of information you have attained will make you a valued commodity in any country you would move to next. Your next venture, be it your own business or an organization to which you offer your skills, will benefit from it.

My recent experience traveling to Istanbul opened my eyes to the perspective of the locals living there. Walking along the Bosphorous and seeing many families there gave me a flashback of what Singapore used to be when I was growing up. Istanbul would see a demographic change as more youths would grow up and change the country. Apart from the official narrative of sky-high inflation, something caught my attention. This development was the brand new

Galataport. Galataport was a Cruise Port at the edge of the Bosphorous, and the Turkish government was building a brand new office hub along with many retail shops. This new development reminds me a lot about these urban projects built in Singapore. One such project developed here was known as Tampines Hub, formerly a sports recreational hub where people would come to swim and play certain sports. About a decade ago, the government decided to launch a brand new concept of changing the sports hub into a mega hub. The mega hub would consist of the same sports activities, F&B joints, and many retail outlets.

I spent my morning walking around the brand-new Galataport to see the crowd and assess the situation. One key observation I've had was that the prices of the stuff sold there were higher than the local tea I could have a few blocks down on the streets of Istanbul. The food was more hygienic and had a more professional feel, with teams wearing uniforms and service staff deployed. Surprisingly, most of the staff spoke English, which I surmised must have been a requirement for people to be employed there.

The scenes there during weekends and weekdays were different. On weekends, it was packed everywhere with locals and international people. Trying to find a seat in a restaurant there on weekends was an impossible task. On weekdays, it was different. The morning was empty; during the afternoon, few people were having lunch, and in the evenings, it was dead silent. The idea suddenly popped into my head that this project of turning the Galataport into a massive urban attraction wouldn't happen overnight. This project would be a long-term play by the Turkish government. The office space above the shops was still empty and not occupied. There will come a time when the offices will get leased, and the shops beneath prosper from it. Give it five-ten years from now, and Galataport would become different. The real estate surrounding Galataport would go through the roof, and the demand would skyrocket. That was the first thought that came to my mind. The location was also perfect; it was a stone's throw away (a 20-minute walk) from the old city of Sultanahmet, home of the Hague Sophia and Blue Mosque. Being located in the heart of Beyoglu meant that going to other touristy destinations such as Isketal Street, Taksim Square, and Galata Tower could be accomplished. Besiktas and the Asian Side of Istanbul were also easily accessible with this central location.

The above is the information I gather from going abroad, spotting trends in their own country abroad, and the desired outcome. Turkey might implement a combination of business and digital nomad visas to attract more people to Istanbul. Their current citizenship program saw its requirement of USD 250,000 go up to USD 400,000 for property investment - signaling that investors who saw the same opportunity as me have already made their move.

This example is one of the more "rogue" methods of acquiring capital and getting value out of it is traveling. Nothing expands your worldview more than traveling and living abroad. There's a quote by Jim Rogers, "The best investors moved to France in 1810s, New York in 1910s, and Asia in the 2010s."

My acquaintances over the year have treated traveling as some sort of vacation. When they visit a country, they do not visit neighborhoods where the locals live and walk around the CBD. You can learn so much by spending a day walking a business district. Do the working class there drink a lot of coffee? Are there Starbucks and Mcdonald's on every street corner? Where do these people go after work? What is their working culture? One can learn about the country through the habits of its population.

Traveling is more than just visiting touristy areas and snapping a few quick Instagram pictures to get that dopamine high. One of the upsides of technology is using it to connect with people of the same interests as you in the country you visit. Let's say you are an entrepreneur looking to expand overseas. A few clicks on your phone and scheduling a meetup with the top business lawyer in the country is within your grasp - compared to spending an entire day looking through directories of office buildings. Have a quick chat with the lawyer, pay the fee for his time and consultation, and you have made more use of your time abroad than 99% of the people who travel for "leisure."

How about the outskirts? What commodities do these countries produce the most? Going to Vietnam, I've seen the blooming Vietnamese Coffee industry - an extremely underrated investment area for many. Rice fields populate the countryside, and the profession of being a farmer has a good reputation. In Japan, you can see individual farmers rearing their cows with love.

You can attain more wealth and knowledge by spending four years going through the roughest terrains in rural parts of the world (deemed as third-world) than in college studying for a degree under the tutelage of a professor who spent his entire life in academia.

As you have noticed in the past two years, the world seems to be moving in one direction. Even you! The disgruntled and vigilant capitalists have seen something strange with your friends and families. They seem to not care too much about certain liberties being taken away from them in real-time. The Covid-19 pandemic wasn't so much about the virus seemingly appearing and killing a small population of the world - the governments and their response to it was the trojan horse that didn't seem to make most people bat an eye.

Changing your environment has become an ordeal. With a mandate centrally coordinated by the WHO, governments carried out their orders and swiftly shut down the world. Airlines went bust, and airports became empty.

That means that being able to relocate and go from one country to another is being suppressed gradually. The nearby hour trip by plane is going to become incredibly scarce soon. Your dream of moving to another continent to experience a different side of reality is getting taken away.

A capitalist's dream of acquiring multiple passports and establishing various businesses on the globe is getting limited as some countries have bowed down the iron hand of the central planners.

One thing that keeps me going is a quote an elder gentleman shared with me while we were talking about traveling. His body became frail, and the chance of him traveling wasn't an option anymore.

"Travel as much as you can while you are still young. You won't know when you won't be able to."

For as long as traveling is possible in this time of massive chaos, capitalize as much as possible. Travel far and wide and enjoy everything that this world has to offer. The goal is to see as much as you can. When you finally experience a country worth living in - regardless of business or relocation purposes, craft a plan and execute it. If your goal is to be a sovereign man, try to place yourself on as many grids as possible - multiple passports, driving licenses, foreign trusts, and businesses everywhere. Your ability to control the environment is an understated asset. Act fast and act now.

Control of your health

One can have all the money in the world. But without a properly functioning body, what is all that money used other than it used in the medical cartel system?

I wasn't the most active person to those who knew me back in the public school education system. Often I would get a doctor's demo to avoid the P.E class (Physical education, something like the exercise class), and I hated the idea of playing ball games and running and needing to change out to my uniform after that. Since that, I've avoided exercising like the plague. My actions led to me gaining a lot of weight, reaching 96 kilograms (211 pounds) at nineteen years old! Constant trips to the clinic became part of my youth as I found myself getting ill often. My enlistment into the Singapore Armed Forces as part of the mandatory National Service for all Singaporean males saved me from this perpetual self-destructive habit. My confidence in my physical health went from zero to a hundred. I would progress from being able to do only ten pushups to a hundred by the end of a month in the army camps. My running speed gradually got better, but the one exercise that plagued me for life - the pull-ups - was something I couldn't do no matter what. It wasn't until I entered the Air Force that I met my close squadron mates, which led to us often going for runs and to the gym together during our spare time.

One day as we watched a new cohort of sergeants post into our unit, a fellow unit friend was scrolling through Instagram at the time and mentioned that one of these new sergeants was a fitness model.

That piqued our curiosity, and we eventually sought out that fitness model sergeant. He gave us advice at the gym - exercises to be done, tracking calories and nutrients, and proper forms for each type of exercise. That led to me hitting the gym regularly, even after my days in National Service. The day I was finally able to do one pull-up made me smile like a child who had gotten a candy bar. It was a significant milestone in my fitness journey.

With a very disciplined and strict approach to my fitness, I would exercise twice a day - once in the morning when I would go for a swim and then some strength training in the afternoon at the gym. Most won't have the time to exercise twice a day, but if you do, I highly recommend it.

One big lesson I learned was that nobody cares about you more than you would care about yourself. I learned this the hard way when I used to have terrible skin, leading to crazy acne popping up everywhere on my face. A combination of terrible sleeping habits, lack of exercise, and drinking too much bubble tea (with its processed sugars) led to my frequent acne breakouts.

My acne problem was a big issue during my teenage days; most people who had it would spiral to significantly low self-esteem. Fortunately, I wasn't too phased about it as I was naturally confident in myself - having become a card game champion and several other accomplishments early on. My parents were more concerned with my acne problem than I was. My mother would get me the best skin doctor money could buy, and regular sessions with him were scheduled quarterly for consultation and diagnosis.

These sessions with the dermatologist were not cheap. It wasn't something a regular Joe in Singapore could afford, and my mother didn't faze at that revelation. Nothing is as strong as a mother's love for her child, and she couldn't stand to see me look unattractive. For years, under this dermatologist's guidance, I would take multiple creams and medications to "solve" this acne problem of mine. The problem stagnated, and nothing was progressing. My skin still looked terrible, with my doctor trying to convince me that it "takes time." I decided to take it into my own hands to solve this problem once and for all.

A couple of changes happened during my college days and my journey into the adult world of work - I began to see the fruits of my labor after five years of constant exercise and proper dieting. Being particular with the food I've eaten since young, combined with my strict fitness regime that spawned from my days as a soldier, made my skin start to clear up. I was no longer going to bed at three in the morning and only had four hours of sleep daily. I stopped staying up late to meet acquaintances for supper. Carbonated Soft Drinks and the bubble tea habit were gone. My meals consist of tons of vegetables, seafood, and some meat. Hydration was also integral, and I found myself drinking tons of water.

The medicines and consultations were a placebo that had no effect, and I went cold turkey on it for a year. One year passed, and I had a consultation with my dermatologist; he was pleased to see my skin getting better. What he said next was.

"Wow! It looks like my medicine is finally working. Your skin has gotten better. Congratulations!"

I looked at the man with a cold poker face and chuckled. Deep down, I was disgusted with this so-called top dermatologist. For years he was swindling money from my mother, wasting our time, and constantly promoting a line of pharmaceutical products down my throat. It was at that moment that I had an epiphany - if my problem was a small one like a skin problem, what happens if someone else has a problem they face such as cancer or diabetes, what if the doctor in charge of them gave them the same treatment as I received? That was a tough pill to swallow and opened my eyes to the world of the medical system.

To understand the medical system, one needs to look at things objectively. On a micro level, the medical system consists of doctors (specialists, surgeons, general practitioners), nurses, and administrative staff. These workers operate based on their worldview - be it wanting to be in the medical system to help others, to earn a lot of money, and to fulfill their Asian parent's dream of becoming one. Everyone has motivations and desires based on the kind of programming they have received from birth. On a macro level, the medical system is the same as the logistics system, the F&B system, and every other system that makes up the overall hierarchy - an organization, a business model. A hospital may have a brand that goes with the tagline "For the public" or "Giving public healthcare to the masses," but it doesn't change the fact that it is a business. Businesses operate on rationality, not emotions. The workers in the medical system may have their emotional reasons for being part of this system, but in the grand scheme of things, they're just replaceable cogs in this machine. A business's goal is to generate cash flow. So the doctor you meet regularly deep down cares about you. The bigger picture always looms behind him whenever he attends his monthly, quarterly, or annual reviews - how much revenue did they generate for the business? Hence, you see the doctor always trying to garner your sympathy by being very sympathetic towards your illness and pushing pharmaceutical drugs to purchase.

There's a duality to the doctor's dilemma. On one side, they serve you based on their desires. On the other side, doctor ensures that to carry on their mission of being health hero, they schedule several consultations and medications as part of their "job's requirements." Failure to do so will lead to the doctors facing a terrible performance review and the risk of losing their jobs.

In a sense, the medical system is as good as a Spotify subscription. TLDR, the healthcare business system, is a subscription-based one.

Fast forward to today, the Covid-19 vaccination program carried out worldwide is a cause for concern. Since I laid out the healthcare subscription business model, the vaccination program has become the ultimate business model for the medical system. With governments signing on and pledging to fight Covid-19, they have become the basis for the demand curve for this vaccine.

What happens is that governments become supporters of this demand-supply curve by using the national budget to buy up these vaccines for the population to take. The Covid-19 vaccine has become a scheduled vaccination program and doesn't consist of just one vaccine - it is two, three, and at this rate, has become infinity! The vaccination program means that the healthcare companies creating this vaccine would see recurring revenue for their products and a boost to their balance sheets due to the government working in their favor. Hospitals and health agencies would also see a rise in demand for their job roles. Since healthcare has become a nationalized institution, it would only lead to one thing - more government spending and higher inflation and taxation for all. However, just buying the vaccine isn't enough for the governments to encourage their population to take it. Governments worldwide, taking orders from the WHO, mandated the vaccine for their citizens; not taking it would strip citizens of their human rights in society. The combination of the public-private partnership becoming the demand driver and the government's ability to sign new laws; means that the healthcare and medical system's reign of profits is here to stay.

I'm laying this out as a precursor because an individual's health is integral to retaining their sovereignty. Your control over your finances is easy, environment as well when you have your finances in check. But when it comes to health, it is more of a discipline thing. Everyone knows vaccines have side effects and could harm some individuals after taking them. In some cases, people drop dead after being administered it.

Despite these facts, one would choose not to take it, citing their health as a reason. But the general public doesn't care about your choices; your sovereign right to your body isn't necessary for a democracy. Democracy is as such; the group is more important than the individual. You choose not to take it? Then say goodbye to your rights. Mandating a vaccine results in that. Governments simply do what the majority wants; not doing so would render them not getting elected in the next election for that political party.

Your health is at risk when the majority demands a collective response to a crisis. I can touch my heart and predict that there will come a time when you will no longer have the right over what health program the government wants you to participate in to "uphold democracy." One day, governments would mandate a health program to "sanitize you," not participating in this program would lead a Roachie Bot 3.3 to your doorstep to coerce you into submission. Boston Dynamics style, I would say.

What's in those vaccines and regular health screening? I wouldn't go into detail here as most sci-fi movies have already shown you the future.

How to capitalize on events?

It isn't all doom and gloom regarding the "smart" future approaching us in lockstep. As cliche as it may sound, when there is darkness, there is also light. As the central planners make their plans accessible for the general public to see, few would even bother to pay any attention to them.

You can always count on humanity to dismiss anything that goes against their socially manufactured worldview as a conspiracy theory. As recent as the Covid-19 pandemic, investors who could see the writing on the wall started selling off all of their stock holdings before February 2020. By the end of March 2020, we saw a total bloodbath as the stock market crashed to the floor. It isn't luck that made these investors sell it early when they saw a crisis coming - it was the instinct in them - honed by years of ignoring the noise and focusing on things that truly mattered.

What happened after the rebound when the stock market went to the moon after March 2020? It became a tale as old as time itself. The bewildered herd, the general population, started pumping their money into the stock market. Tech, biotech, and anything under the sun saw their valuation go through the roof. Everyone believed the mainstream media's view that Covid-19 made Tech stocks valuable, but the truth was far more sinister. The insane money printing and stimulus checks were the reason the stock market went up. Investing gurus all over Youtube gained followers as an artificial bull market started - any stock that these gurus recommended went up, and they gained a cult-like following.

When I had my morning tea back when I was still working full-time, there was always talk by my colleagues about the hot stock to buy, how to get rich quickly, and the best cryptocurrency to buy. I was still inexperienced regarding market cycles - its tops and bottoms - my first stock mania and the first time I started investing.

It was comfortable seeing everything I invested in going up. I thought I was a genius, every altcoin I bought on a decentralized exchange instantly doubled in value. During the month I gave my resignation letter in 2021, I decided to sell off the majority of my stocks and cryptocurrency. I don't call it luck; I would call it a calculated decision because I was expecting a measly 8% gain annually and everything having astronomical amounts of wealth in less than a year was something I could not fathom. Most of my stocks were up, and my cryptocurrencies went through the roof. Inner paranoia and the need to constantly check my phone kept me in fear, even though my paper net worth was high for a young adult. That's when I decided I had enough of it, the food business was more important to me in the next few months, and I didn't want to have my attention span solely on digital money.

The next few months saw topsy-turvy events that resulted in a massive crash in every market. The inflation crisis started, the Ukraine-Russia conflict and the Fed decided to raise interest rates. Every unprepared investor lost their shirts, and it was clear we were in for a ride. Investing Gurus became exposed for the frauds they were as they held on to the credibility left after every stock recommended dropped by nearly half of its valuation. The blockchain enthusiasts were wiped out and remained silent. The massive investing bubble had popped, and I just watched as the events played out. One day when you see many people talking about investing and random nobodies living in their mother's basements telling you which dog coin to buy - you know we have reached a market top.

My financial journey didn't end there. Taking a close friend's recommendation, I started listening to a gentleman named Peter Schiff. Schiff is an economist, and a business owner, which gave him credibility not only as an expert in the financial markets but also meant that his predictions were worth to listen. He was one of the biggest proponents of purchasing commodities and overseas foreign stocks - advice that most gurus never give as they all seem to favor their biotech and tech stocks. Given his thoughts on the supply of commodities that could not match the crazy money printing, it meant that we were in for a massive bull market in commodities. As always, I took a grain of salt and listened on. As the stock market took a dump, I decided to take his advice and put a small percentage of my portfolio into those sectors.

At the start of 2022, as everyone saw their portfolios ravaged, my portfolio went up. Not by a long shot, but uncommon during a period when people turned instant bear. The accuracy of his predictions startled me, and I started to pay more heed to his analysis and forecast for the whole of 2022. Slowly, I started to pay attention and tune in to other economists and financial experts who received the same treatment as Schiff had. From the mainstream media point of view, Peter Schiff wasn't given any time of day due to his always recommending investment advice deemed as outlandish and going against the growth stock narrative. The biggest thing that made the investing guru community hate Schiff with their life is his anti-bitcoin sentiment. Schiff made statements years ago that established himself as Bitcoin's greatest enemy - citing its uselessness and the massive mania that caused young people to go into it - it sounded more like the biggest Ponzi scheme to him.

Going through the Youtube channel owned by Peter Schiff, I started to go through some of his older videos, and not surprisingly - he was spot on regarding issues in the 2008 housing crash, having predicted its fallout from 2005-2006. One insight of his was his belief in buying into commodities producers, mining, and natural resources during the dip of March 2020, when the Covid-19 market crash happened. When the dust settled, the audience who diligently listened to his analysis and insights were up nearly 1000% since, while the majority saw less than 100% gains in their overpriced tech stocks.

The call he made was the money printing via stimulus checks combined with the lockdowns all over the world would cause the supply of natural resources and energy to dwindle - partly due to the number of people working in these sectors forced to stay home and collect these checks. One day when the demand was to increase with lockdowns removed and people returning to their lives again, the current supply would not be able to meet the new surge in demand.

Another part of his call was the latest green movement that the climate warriors (and soon-to-be citizens of smart cities) demonizing the gas of life - carbon. Unfortunately, emotions don't do well in an environment of reality and rationality. Sanctions and the climate warriors begging for the government to do something about the demonic oil & gas industry meant that the cost of producing natural resources would increase due to increased government intervention. These climate warriors refuse to acknowledge reality, and their virtue signaling caused the insane sky-high price hikes faced worldwide.

Touch your heart and ask yourself the following questions.

Do your friends discuss natural resources supply and what would happen when you have lockdowns?

What topics are the people you hang out with discussing?

Is there a friend in your circle who can see through the illusion of reality and mention the liberties being taken away in real time?

When a random guy down the street gives you advice regarding investing, you know it's time to sell. Fortunately, I have a friend in the oil & gas sector, and often I would hear what he has to say - how dirty the industry is with the hard work and the amount of government intervention he has to go through to get one job done. Not many people have the luxury of having close friends working in a lucrative sector such as this, and through conversations with him, I could understand the larger picture of the world. Spending time with acquaintances once in a while, the topics of investing and personal finances would come up. Never has there been another person apart from that friend who would talk about oil & gas, and that's when I know it is still a good play for investing.

The ultimate tool a capitalist has at his disposal - SPECIALIZED KNOWLEDGE. There is a reason heads of noble families would pay high amounts of legal currency to acquire the services of a professional - be it a master chef, a top lawyer, the best accountant of their land, or even the best fitness trainer available. Specialized knowledge only possessed by the best is what makes a capitalist go to another level above the random cafe owner in Singapore. My friend, whose family owns an oil & gas company, can advise me in this sector and has helped me tremendously.

Look at your friends beside you, the areas they invest in, and the type of stuff they do regularly. These aren't specialized tools that a capitalist can use to make themselves rich - these are the habits of ham & eggers. What is a ham & egger? When you look at the construction of a sandwich, what is in the middle? That's right. It's the ham and eggs. The kind of hobbies and habits that the ham & egger is the same across the board.

They do the same thing. These groups of people buy the same overpriced public housing project because their worldview is limited to a tiny island such as Singapore. They invest in the S&P 500 as the "stock market always goes up." They also buy Bitcoin and Ethereum when the news pumps it into the headlines. Nobody gets rich by mimicking the trades of ham & eggers; the most one would get out of it is what you call the middle class - the ham and eggs of a sandwich.

A simple rule of thumb is - you don't want to take advice from someone you would not trade places with - a piece of advice I received since young. The people with specialized knowledge wouldn't trade information with you unless they deem you an equal. More often than not, they would be as silent as mice and go about their day. Conversations would never take place unless they deem you worthy of their time. Becoming a specialist in your craft would take years, and there's always a price to pay for it.

Many would tell you to invest in this and that. But there's only one way for an individual to navigate the waters of these troubling times - networking. Capital has a specific use when one knows where to allocate it. Through networking, one can equip themselves with knowledge and share it with individuals worthy of their time.

Remember that your network mirrors your life and the value you bring to society. Their knowledge can make or break their circle.

What can a man my age do about "The Great Reset" coming to our doorsteps in 2030, a projection made by the central planners in NGOs such as the WEF and UN (United Nations)? I believe that good intentions always end with catastrophic outcomes for the ones planning it and the benefactors (the general population) when their goal doesn't materialize as planned. Commodities shortages have become a factor post-Covid-19, resulting in the craziest inflation most youths have seen. Imagine a future where the sustainable goals and the so-called net-zero dream materializes - there will be cockroach burgers and soy lattes - most of the things consumed as food will become synthetic.

Our current generation of being desk-bound and being fed GMO foods has less than a century of history - who knows what kind of side effects await us?

Living Off Grid

There has been a significant movement by the pro-freedom crowd (usually associated with the Bitcoin/freedom gang) to become sovereign, with the ultimate sign of being sovereign being to grow your food. The "grow your own food" mentality has spun up a whole wave of interest with the amount of content being created digitally on YouTube and blogs. The entire premise is to live somewhere with abundantly rich natural resources, build your own home, cultivate your crops, and live your life there till you die.

I have a friend who enjoys talking about how everyone should move abroad, somewhere as far away from cities - preferably in the outskirts - and just buy a plot of land, build a home, and then grow their food. Problem solved. You are in control of your own life and finally able to beat the system. These conversations have become more common, especially with the Covid-19 appearance and the government's collective draconian measures of lockdowns and forcing people to stay indoors. More and more people have moved to towns and decided to live out their lives there in nature.

In the previous chapter where I hypothesized the future of one with smart cities and the old world is just that. The humans that believe in the mainstream narrative of climate change and sustainability have moved into the smart cities, essentially the technological outcome that the central planners want - the ultimate grid of control. Those who chose to live outside the grid decided to live outside the cities by living outskirts. In a sense, the need for cities came about when people realized the ease of access to just living in a densely populated environment. Healthcare, food, water, and essentials to living become accessible by relocating to a city. Having been outskirts in several countries, it is not fun not having a toilet at every corner and water available for purchase at a convenience store.

That's a sacrifice that the pro-freedom crowd must swear to uphold - giving up their instant gratification to supplies in exchange for being in control over their lives. Unfortunately, this will be impossible. The ones living outskirts have lived that way since they were born, like the educational system that programs the youths in countries to live and act a certain way, the community where the townfolks have their version of education. Many would leave their towns for city life, citing the lack of opportunities available in their small towns. To move back to the outskirts for freedom sounds like a catch-22 scenario. In the future, considering that humanity has always taken the path of least resistance, I believe that most people would give up on their freedoms for the smart cities, assimilating themselves into the hive mind instead of leaving their destiny in their hands.

From the perspective of my friend, who enjoys talking about moving off-grid, it sounds like a fantastic idea. It's the same as everyone who talks about doing "XYZ," but then there's no action plan to get it started. Growing your food and sharing your harvests sound noble, but there will always be bottom-feeders in every society. City dwellers who "achieved" success from their useless jobs tend to think things are that easy everywhere else. Just because you got a good grade in an annual performance review does not translate to your labor of growing crops. Their worldview is so narrow that it is almost laughable. My first job as a teen has exemplified (Chapter 2) shown professionals avoiding their job to seem busy while the rest would shoulder the work assigned to them.

One example is the community garden on the estate I live in, where there are vegetables, flowers, and even fruits are grown there. A group of gardeners comprising my mother and her friends would actively contribute to the garden's crops by providing seeds and taking turns to water them. My gardening team would distribute the harvests amongst themselves and sparked an interest in some neighbors to join the gardening team. Reality doesn't pan out as expected, and these interested neighbors ended up being interested in one thing - only wanting the harvests without putting in the effort. Coming early before the gardening team would meet and collect their fruits and vegetables, this group of savages would bring their scissors and help themselves to as much of the harvest as they desired before the gardening team had the chance to collect their spoils! Sometimes they would destroy the plot of land with their acts and then feign innocence by lying through their teeth. There was a time when I grew some vegetables, and when it was time to harvest them, some savage took my entire pot of vegetables and brought it home!

That is the kind of experience I had when it came to having a community, and most wouldn't experience them until they venture off-grid and start growing their food. Remember that in the off-grid scenario, you would be living in, there won't be any police you can call to rescue you. Some people who moved off-grid tend to have individualistic and eccentric behavior associated with them; one wrong argument and that individual wouldn't mind whipping out his knife to dice you up. If there's one thing I'm betting on, I will always bet on the human instinct to mess things up.

There is also the wildlife issue - how are you - the human that only knew how to trade stocks and type on Reddit - going to deal with a rampaging bear or swarm of insects that want to devour all the crops you have? Unless you have prepared to live off-grid, go ahead. If you don't have a Plan C to your Plan B, I suggest you think twice about it.

For as long as an individual still relies on the SWIFT system, they cannot escape the grid - or the smart grid when it becomes deployed - the CBDC system will be the ultimate system when it goes online. Not every country will be part of the smart grid; look at some of the "poorest" or third-world ones (whatever constitutes them as third-world), and you will conclude that these countries might end up as the lands savages of the old world will live. There are some countries that one can move to which aren't that "developed" and "woke" - mainly due to the lack of investments and foreign interventions from the central planners. Eastern Europe comprises the Czech Republic, Slovakia, and Hungary, to name a few, and has seen popularity for liberty-seeking individuals living in Western Europe.

Dubai and the gulf states have also become popular due to their favorable taxes and social stability they learned from Singapore. The term "social stability" is frowned upon - some look at the poverty levels in cities such as Dubai and would often cite the treatment these locals receive as "human rights violations" for their hard labor. Funny enough, it doesn't seem to be a problem for those who live there. In a capitalistic society, there are winners and losers. As long as you are winning, someone else is losing.

The only alternative is communism, which we saw a century ago with the gulags and forced labor. We all know how that tale ended. Unfortunately, the history textbooks in Singapore don't show the atrocities in the gulags. Instead, it only talks about the five-year plans and collectivization. No wonder history always repeats itself since no one learns from it.

One possible solution is to live the life of an eternal tourist, a popular profession of choice for westerners fed up with their corporate slave life, and figured out that traveling and making money from it sounds like a great idea. The eternal tourist is a vagabond, owning nothing and being happy, with no assets and only a backpack strapped to his back. One wrong move in some country whose language they don't speak and the vagabond's life ends.

Nobody knows who they are, and to be honest, no one cares. They contribute nothing to society, hopping around from country to country for "different cultural experiences" with locals living in those lands. Does that sound like an ideal life to you? With no roots to call home, no feat worthy of being remembered by, it's a sort of escapism that millennials face. Eventually, the hive mind will assimilate them into their ranks. Their payment processors, the YouTube platform, and even the currency they use still belong to the system - so much for "living life on their terms."

The Capitalist and the average Joe

When you look at history and the lessons learned, there will always be a conflict somewhere. Capitalist, with their capital ready at their disposal, knows the moves to execute when conflict is imminent. The masses are dumbed down, having their instincts controlled by the mainstream media press, and cannot act rationally. Many choose to stay and fight, attending riots and participating in strikes, rallying each other to fight till the bitter end. One can see this behavior in the latest Sri Lanka crisis and the Russia-Ukraine conflict.

Joe chose the path of emotion.

The capitalist chose the path of rationality.

Joe stays to fight the oppressors while the capitalist assesses the situation and executes the move, like a professional card game champion. With the citizens of the countries united against the government for their failed policy, Joe truly believes in the power of the people as they display their collective intention to stand up to tyranny.

The capitalist picks up his phone and gives a phone call to a business associate in Singapore.

"Bro, I got an issue over here. I would need some assistance."

"Yes, I heard about it from my assistant. Go to the location now - everything is ready."

Within minutes, the capitalist walks out of their home. Their immediate loved ones were informed where and when to meet. Having one last glass of purified water in their kitchen, the capitalist bids farewell to his mansion; who knows if he will ever step foot in there again? The chauffeur takes the capitalist to a military base - a private jet awaits him.

The pilot of the private jet greets the capitalist and takes off toward Singapore. The capitalist didn't have to go through immigration, as his assistant settled everything. The capitalist and his family make their way to their penthouse situated in a quiet corner of Singapore, overlooking East Coast Park. With lunch scheduled at the nearby Italian restaurant, the capitalist makes his way there to meet their business associate as a gesture for his swift response and assistance.

Living on as many grids as possible

The idea of living in one country, settling down there, and calling it your home is a concept as old as time itself. However, with recent events shaping up, it is impossible to get a sense of safety and security with governments ramping up their control over the people.

The average Joe - the neighbors you have and the friendly convenience shop owner down the road - has his roots in the country you live in for at least two generations. If anything were to happen to their country, they would stand up and fight for their rights. A crisis doesn't occur overnight; it is often years and even decades of planning by the central planners and the governments. What seems like a benevolent public policy that will benefit the good of its citizens often presents itself as a trojan horse - usually funded by taxation or money printing. This trojan horse will start small until it balloons up.

When the Trojan Horse suddenly becomes a reality, it is often too late for the average Joe to realize. Joe knows that only to fight; his neighbors and brothers-in-arms would rally together to show the government who is boss. Little did the average Joe realize that public policy was something that his parent's generations willingly agreed to via their vote.

The problems the current generation of each country suffers from are the same choices the previous generation made. That's a fact of life that is often understated. Many people never leave their home nests; instead to stay put and hope that things turn out for the best. This Covid-19 response by my fellow Singaporeans has shown me how the mob reacts to scenarios. Less than a handful of Singaporeans I know have rational thoughts about Covid-19, the fear and uncertainty set in, and they believe this virus can potentially kill them. The ones who could see through it knows it can't be that bad. The problem with Covid-19 isn't so much dying from the virus or getting it and then suffering from a bad case of flu; it's the fact that government control has reached a point in this era that it could potentially control every movement of your life.

Henry Kissinger once said.

"Who controls the food supply controls the people; who control the energy can control whole continents; who controls money can control the world."

Looking at the average Joe has no control over the money supply in his life. They are a salaried employee. One wrong move and their financial tap get cut off. Staying and fighting, showing the government who's the boss - merely a fool's attempt to solve problems.

One lesson from history is that trying to solve a government's big problems isn't as simple as showing civil disobedience and rioting. Some may have noble intentions and commit their lives to "serving the public" and trying to fix the country's problems. History has shown that you can do that, but good times only last for a decade or two before it all goes down the drain again. You can always count on humans to mess things up. The government can't help you because they can't even help themselves. YOU can only help yourself. There is no point in being a dissident in your country and showing your anti-government antics; the better way is to avoid tying yourself up with any government and live life on your terms - legally.

The path of a Capitalist is different. It is one I currently walk, the ones my grandfathers took as well - when they decided to leave their home ground for better prospects upon hearing the rallying cry of Lee Kuan Yew to build a new Singapore. Capitalists have the means and a worldwide network that makes their life easier, to keep their families safe from all kinds of trouble when there's blood on the streets.

Honing your craft makes life easier for a capitalist; one can seek employment in another continent by offering his skills, and setting up a business abroad with your history of success is also an option. Even donating capital to a country to acquire residency or citizenship is a move most capitalists make. The advice of the bewildered herd is to save for retirement by working forever. Get a good job, contribute to your CPF, buy a public housing project that you don't own, and have children that don't listen to you for your "retirement plan" - these are some of the advice regular Joes in Singapore pass around. It is almost laughable when an acquaintance suggests to me buying a public housing project because it is "free," considering all the government incentives for it. It isn't "free" if I have to work and pay the mortgage and utilities. Besides, there is a MOP (Minimum occupancy period) where the home cannot be sold or rented out when bought. This MOP last for a minimum of five years! Any capitalist or real-estate investor will stay away from this horrendous deal.

The advice of a capitalist is to have many experiences, make friends everywhere, and network, then become a valued commodity in terms of specialized knowledge that any country you go to will go to lengths to welcome you. Pushing paper in the civil service and having coffee breaks in the afternoon aren't specialized knowledge.

It takes time and expertise to develop one. It took me a decade of playing card games professionally for people to take my advice and tune into my podcast for my insights. For some, it took them over thirty years to have people listen to them regarding their financial insights and outlook. Things that take time are usually worth it, especially when it comes to building a skillset. Writing this book is one way for me to finally turn my skill of writing articles for my card-game blog ten years ago to the next level. Depending on where you live, the career path you are taking, and the business you run. The future that will come with smart cities and the CBDC should be the number one priority in your life. Knowing what's to come will enable you to navigate and look for opportunities to invest and allocate capital, boosting your existing net worth and giving you more financial control. Staying true as a capitalist will enable you to move around different countries and continents. Next, you can acquire residencies and passports (if your current citizenship allows) so that no one government can control your moment when they decide to lock down again.

Once you have both areas covered, you are finally in control of your health - mentally and physically. In an ideal country, access to wild-caught seafood and free-range poultry would replace the farm-bred horrors of a congested city in your life. Being surrounded by fruits and vegetables, free from plantation pesticides and genetically modified substances, would boost your health to the next level. Your mental state would be at peace; without the roar of the woke crowd begging for more government help and your family safely next to you in an environment without chaos.

That is until history repeats itself in your new environment, and your child needs to take the steps they need - as a Rogue Capitalist.

Conclusion

"What do you want to be when you grow up?"

That's a question often tossed around amongst the youths in schools. I firmly believe that my generation (the final batch of millennials before Gen-Z) was the one where we truly wished to do something that was not socially engineered.

Having wanted to be a professional wrestler since I was young, just like my childhood hero Chris Jericho and Kurt Angle, until I realized I wasn't "big enough" in my teens made me focus on the one thing I was good at - playing cards.

Years of honing my skills and being in solitude, taking a path seldom traveled by other Singaporeans, allowed me to view the world from a completely different angle. My sensory abilities cultivated from watching every micro-movements by my opponents sitting across me in championships and my perceptive mindset have turned me into a "big picture" person since my youth.

After finally becoming Champion in the card game I was playing at the time, I was happy - for a mere second. The sudden realization of going from the predator hunting down big name after big name in the professional scene turned me into the prey; other young hungrier talents were constantly analyzing my play patterns and wanted the title I now hold. At the age of seventeen, it was another brutal red pill

I had to swallow - the responsibility of a man who reached the top of his industry has no friends, for everyone is now a potential enemy who wouldn't show you mercy anymore.

I was finally in the shoes of my esteemed neighbors, entrepreneurs, and top professionals in their field - they often hung around each other - seldom spending time with their acquaintances in their respective industries. The only "friends" a professional has been with other top professionals, those who finally reached the top, and what made their bond stronger than steel was their shared experience of going through hell to reach their final destination.

Having my goal of becoming a Champion accomplished in two short years, I set my sights on other adventures to broaden my human experience. From starting blogs to writing about card games I've played to eventually starting my podcast, I was able to share my expertise and thoughts regarding professional card games. I've also traveled alone to different parts of the world, joined the tech industry and been an employee to experience the 9-5 lifestyle, and finally became a businessman myself - an entrepreneur like the mentors I've had. Nothing enriches the soul more than enjoying the absolute wonders that the world has to offer - only attainable with the risk and capital that one has acquired through labor and risk-taking.

With Covid-19 appearing seemingly suddenly to the masses, things have taken a drastic turn for the world. In my parent's generation, things changed rapidly during the 9/11 incident. For my grandparent's generation, it was the 1971 Nixon shock when the dollar went off the gold standard. There is always a massive overhaul in the system that appears once every generation and the entire human race goes through a "Great Reset" - for lack of better terminology. The luxuries as a child I had growing up in Singapore will no longer be accessible to the youths. That is democracy at its finest; rule of the minority by the majority. Running a business in the worst of times can open the time to the truth for the entrepreneur faster than getting destroyed in divorce court. With the number of regulations and restrictions mandated to stop the spread of Covid-19 - our liberties have seemingly disappeared. Believing in the collective will to save their own lives from Covid-19, some would even willingly trample upon the individual's ideals as being selfish and a threat to "our" public health.

Fear and uncertainty have clouded the minds of humanity, and the Covid-19 vaccination program introduced showed the ugly side of democracy. For the longest time, we had seen the good side of it; the only other drastic side of government that the collective consciousness has experienced was communism - the USSR in Russia. The population divided into two; more started to fall in line and embraced the vaccination program even though they didn't want to take it. The individual's morals were cast aside to be part of the mob, for not taking the vaccine meant being alienated and losing the "friends" and corporate handcuffs essential to living the Singaporean dream. The side hanging on to their beliefs slowly choked into submission until March 2022, when the public health bureaucracies eased away into the sunset.

The mob celebrated their victory over Covid-19 and praised everyone for their collective effort in fighting Covid-19 together. The mob's anger at the other side for hanging on to their beliefs evaporated within hours. Life has gone back to normal, and they didn't care about those who stood up for themselves. With the next crisis being an international affair between Russia and Ukraine, the new topic became sky-high inflation, with the Putin price hike being the new boogieman. And as expected, the mob fell for it, hook, line, and sinker. The mainstream media propaganda machine worked during the Donald Trump slander campaign, as it did to make everyone fear Covid-19, and it worked wonders with Vladimir Putin once again.

The lessons I learned from running a food business during these times and going through the cycles of Covid-19 and the insane inflation made me rethink and strategize the outlook as the world heads towards a new era. Running a business in a single location is a naive move for amateurs. The landlord can easily change the rules and regulations and crush your business. Mandating everyone to work from home would render your business insolvent in seconds. Try pissing off the government by playing rogue, and you will have your business gone - licenses revoked and tenancy agreement dissolved. Food no longer has to taste good, all you need is artificial flavoring on top of your frozen GMO meats and pastries, and you are good to go. Pay off a food influencer and a bit of advertising digitally, and people instantly flock to your food business within days.

I still enjoy the experience of enjoying food cooked by legendary Chefs. However, the number of Chefs who source their ingredients is disappearing slowly, with a hive of "get rich quick" wannabe Chefs creating online shops to sell you processed garbage which only destroys your health. The diabetes-inducing creations by circuit bakers constantly affect the dopamine receptors of our minds, turning their consumers into sheep. The rise of circuit bakers and more cafes would expedite the speed of our hawkers getting replaced with these wannapreneurs who would not bat an eye and serve you garbage food.

As I monitor the label on food items, I made it a rule not to purchase anything that has something I do not recognize. Health is underrated, and what you pick into your mouth is starting to become a call for concern with the planned food shortages rearing their ugly head in months. These food shortages are cause-and-effect scenarios from the Russia-Ukraine conflict, and it's more than an international conflict - the effects of the Covid-19 lockdowns worldwide - reducing the current supply of commodities and fertilizers. Like how Covid-19 went away and the mainstream media caused the sheep's attention to turn towards the massive inflation crisis, the next step for our planned collective future of a net-zero climate warrior dream is coming.

During the same week, Singapore announced that Malaysia would start banning the export of fresh chicken, causing a massive uproar from the bewildered herd. The mainstream media reported in the news that a brand new lab to cultivate chicken would be starting its operations here. Lab-grown chicken, how disgusting does that sound? The saying "if it doesn't come out from a living thing, then you shouldn't eat it" is such an accurate statement it hurts my soul to know that this future of dystopian novels and shows I've watched is finally here. Synthetic meats are here to stay; nothing the Average Joe can do about it. When you see the mainstream media propagating that something is happening, you can bet that the governments behind this machine already have a response to it. This problem/reaction scenario has been in the works way before anyone's estimations.

Being a capitalist means that the individual needs to be aware of important things happening in his surroundings. During the 2021 National Day Rally Speech, when most Singaporeans were busy doing nothing, I noticed a line that Prime Minister Lee Hsien Loong mentioned, "The government will create the environment for businesses to succeed." For some, it might sound great - the government is doing its best for entrepreneurs to succeed. For the past few decades, Singapore has become a country that entrepreneurs have chosen to call home. Its reputation, favorable taxes, and currency strength have made it a tier-one choice for businesses. However, that statement got me thinking. Why did he make a statement when the Singaporean government has been doing that since the start? Piecing the speech together gave it a new meaning - the industries and emerging technologies that will be integral to the intelligent city/AI end game - these businesses will be welcome here.

When the synthetic meat lab-grown chicken appeared (the company name is GOOD Meat) and the news was available for all to see, I noticed one odd thing. Rarely do companies take a nice picture with people in it; the main point of taking photographs and featuring them for a relatively unknown company here is to give the public a grasp of their business. However, the picture that caught my attention was one showing the CEO of the synthetic chicken company, along with other bureaucrats. The most crucial bureaucrat in the photo op is the Minister of Sustainability and the Environment. You can't make this stuff up. The synthetic meat, the shortages worldwide, and the net-zero/zero carbon thing are tied together. When one thing ends, another begins.

The F&B industry filled with honorable Chefs will soon become replaced by wannabe Chefs who will take up sponsorships and get coerced by synthetic meat producers to use these fake meats instead of livestock to make a living. These wannabe Chefs would have to bow down to the woke mob for not committing to the carbonless future or risk hurting their ESG score.

The food you put into your mouth is already a big problem with the amount of artificial "food" in restaurants. It doesn't help that the hawker scene (mainly fresh food every day) is choked into early retirement by soulless franchises of chain stores selling you frozen GMO produce. Circuit bakers and popping up of random new bakeries and cafes selling you the same latte and pastries are also part of the problem - the flour, wheat, and artificial sugars used will only harm you while giving you a "dopamine high."

To tie all of this together, the 2022 NDR speech featured a key highlight regarding the repeal of 377a - Gay couples can have legal intercourse. Most would have their opinions; whether they agree or disagree, they must understand that their opinion does not have any weight. The only way to look at this repeal is through the lens of a capitalist - what are the demographic changes to Singapore?

How will it change Singapore ten, twenty, and fifty years from now? The macro picture is looking at Singapore and realizing the eradication of gender roles in real time - males and females both work. Both are equally free in the sexual marketplace. Conservative values no longer hold weight with how weak Singaporean male youths have become. Combined with the synthetic food they consume that affects their DNA structures and the common goal of climate change and sustainability - making a few good calls in some sectors would be a speculative move.

In history, there have been many systems existed. None of them has given humanity a fighting chance at a better quality of life than capitalism. Unfortunately, systems in society have pros and cons; for as long as humanity exists, we will inevitably try to undermine and engage in war with one another. Each cycle lasts roughly 200 years before a cataclysmic event, and things reset.

Since the year 2000, many things have rapidly changed radically. 9/11, the 2008 crash, Covid-19, and now climate change creeping toward its peak of dominance. All of this could only be made possible with the trojan horse known as Technology. The hive mind of Technology, or Big Tech, as it is known today, has assimilated the consciousness of humanity to achieve its end goal of singularity. With the individual conditioned to bow down to the collective, as shown in Covid-19, individual values have become obsolete. Once the hive mind is near its final form, humanity would no longer need to exist other than to carry out the work of the singularity. Humanoids, AI, robots - the era of the machine and humanity's lack of control over their creation would come as foretold in dystopian Sci-Fi novels.

All hope is not lost. Surviving in this era of madness propagated by the insanity of humanity's collective wish for equality would require the individual to go rogue. Every industry known to men is no longer what it was decades ago. Dissent by industry players would result from the heavy hand of the government's might fueled by the cry of the woke mob, crushing the business and rendering them obsolete. The road out of this is capitalism - by understanding the need for free markets - becoming a student of history to pave the way after the imminent collapse to rebuild a brand new society in a hundred, maybe two hundred years from now. The Climate change agenda and AI end game are impossible to derail. The only solution is to plan for what comes after that. That's the role that we, the capitalists, have to shoulder.

The near future of the West looks disastrous. My heart goes out to the ones in the USA and the EU. The smart ones have already moved to Asia.

So what's your next move, fellow Capitalists?

ABOUT THE AUTHOR

Johann Loke is an Entrepreneur, second-generation Restauranteur, Podcaster, Writer, and ex-Software Engineer. He is a Professional Card Game Champion, having competed in the highest levels of multiple professional card games for decades. His experience as a Professional Card Game player has sharpened his mind to perceive and accurately predict macro trends, enabling him to excel in the world of entrepreneurship with wisdom and precision far beyond his age.

www.ingramcontent.com/pod-product-compliance
Lightning Source LLC
Chambersburg PA
CBHW071607150726

48000CB00004B/1618